MILLENNIUM ISLAM

MILLENNIUM ISLAM

Edited by Sheikh Latif Abdul-Malik

Published by
MALICOM

Informal Publication in 1999, United Kingdom
Informal Publication 2000, Middle East
Official Publication 2001, United Kingdom

Published by:
M A L I C O M
PO Box 320,
Oxford,
OX1 1QR
United Kingdom

www.millennium-islam.com
sales@millennium-islam.com

The Editors and all those involved in this project would like to thank all the scholars whose work has been utilised for this book.

Every effort has been made to authenticate the hadith mentioned within this compilation. May our Lord bestow upon us all goodness in this world and in the hereafter.

ISBN 0-9540593-0-1

A catalogue record of this book is available from the British Library.

HQ	=	The Holy Qur'an
(pbuh)	=	May the Peace and Blessings of Allah the Almighty be upon Prophet Muhammad
Sunnah	=	The Way of Prophet Muhammad (pbuh)
hadith	=	An authentic tradition of the Way of the Prophet (pbuh)
Ummah	=	Community, mainly to the Islamic world
inshallah	=	If Allah wills

May Allah be pleased with the Family and Companions of the Prophet (pbuh) and all Muslims of all times and all places.

In the Name of Allah, the Most Compassionate, the Most Merciful,
and in the Name of His Messenger, the Best of Mankind, Muhammad (pbuh)

'There is no god but Allah,
and Muhammad is His Messenger.'
The Declaration of Faith

'In the Name of Allah, The Most Compassionate, The Most Merciful,
Praise be to Allah,
The Lord of the Worlds,
The Most Compassionate, The Most Merciful;
The Master of the Day of Judgement.
You alone do we worship and You alone do we ask for help.
Guide us to The Straight Path,
The Path of those on whom
You have bestowed Your Grace.
Not those who earned Your Anger,
nor of those who went astray.'
The Opening (HQ, 1:1-7)

'Say: He is Allah, The One,
Allah, the Eternal, Absolute;
He begets not, nor was He begotten;
And there is none like unto Him.'
Purity of Faith (HQ, 112:1-4)

'You are the Best of Peoples ever evolved for mankind.
You enjoin what is right and forbid what is wrong
and you believe in Allah.'
(HQ, 3:110)

'Truly, Allah will raise up at the beginning of every century for this people,
one who will renew their religion for them'
Prophet Muhammad (pbuh)

'Allah will send a man from my family who will fill the Earth with equity and justice
as it was previously filled with oppression and tyranny.'
Prophet Muhammad (pbuh)

'Let there be no compulsion in religion.
For Truth has become distinct from Falsehood.'
(HQ, 2:256)

CONTENTS

THE FUTURE OF HOPE : ISLAM

'In a few years.
With Allah is the Command, of the Past and of the Future.
And, on that day, the believers will rejoice.'
(HQ, 30:4)

Everywhere we turn we see miracles. Humans, animals, water - everything is a miracle. Muslims know the Miracle of Allah to be the Holy Qur'an, a book, but no ordinary book. True, it may be on paper and written in ink like millions of other books, but this book is the Final Revelation of Allah. Within it is contained the guidance to being a better person, a Muslim, the person who worships Allah, the Creator of the Worlds. Aisha, may Allah be pleased with her for being one of the beloved wives of the Prophet Muhammad (pbuh) said of him after his death: '**He was the Qur'an in action**.'

The first word revealed to Muhammad (pbuh) by the Archangel Jibril (Gabriel) was 'Iqra' which means 'Read!' The future is not about wars, it is about information, and the best information is knowledge. Muslim scholars through the ages have written volumes on every aspect of life using this word, 'Read!' as the basis for their inspiration. Islam is a force which cannot be 'hijacked' - its Message is universal and the more people that know The Truth, the more can embrace it. Thus, a book recommending the Holy Qur'an and the Sunnah of the Prophet (pbuh) is to be the foundation on which to spread Islam in the Millennium.

This book is addressed to all of Mankind, but its true value lies in the Message to those who are the Best of Mankind, the Ummah of Muslims. It is intended to provide hope and guidance to Muslims, those who submit to Allah, but it also acts as a warning. It is a warning to those who fear Islam becoming the dominant force. Have no fear - Islam will become the dominant force of the future.

The book is also for non-Muslims who are disillusioned with the greed, corruption, moral decay, poverty, evil and hatred that surrounds them. You know that there is a better world out there, where life is better, where people are nice and decent to each other, where the right laws are enforced in the right way, where the rich give to the poor, where man regards his fellow man like his own brother. This book will hopefully show you that better world.

The best weapons of any battle are not the latest in technology - it is always knowledge. The ideas, notions and values that are contained here are those that nobody can ever criticise as a whole - the concept is too strong and the earnest intention is the Truth, and nothing but the Truth. In the history of humanity, the only book to neither be changed nor contain any error is the Holy Qur'an. The simpleton and the intellectual will both be convinced if Allah wills. However, like any other book, it is not what we have read, but what we have learned. The moment we learn, the world will change.

This book is dedicated to Allah, the Provider of Guidance, the Possessor of Majesty and Beauty, and His Messenger, the Best Example of Mankind, and to all Muslims, the Best of Mankind (HQ, 3.110).

'The parable of those who have taken protectors besides Allah is that of the spider which builds a web; but, surely, the frailest of houses is the spider's web, if they but knew.'
(HQ, 29:41)

**'And those who strive in Our Way,
We open pathways for them:
For surely, Allah is with those who do good.'**
(HQ, 29:69)

THE MUSLIMS IN THE MILLENNIUM

The Millennium, the next 1000 years of mankind's future, is a natural time to take control – individually, communally and globally.

Who are we? Why are we here? What is our mission?

Two verses of the Holy Qur'an indicate the nature of Islam in the Millennium:

'Truly, the religion with Allah is Islam.'
(HQ, 3:19)

'Verily, one day with your Lord is a Millennium of your reckoning.'
(HQ, 22:47)

Within this Millennium, Islam will be the largest religion on Earth, the first time it will have more adherents than any other religion, if Allah wills. It is in this Millennium that the Mahdi comes to reinstate the Caliphate of Allah and fills the Earth with justice and prosperity for all. It is this Millennium where the False Messiah, the Anti-Christ, is killed by the Mahdi's successor and dear friend, Jesus the son of Mary, a Muslim and one of Allah's Prophets (may the peace of Allah be upon him). It is this Millennium where the Earth becomes the Islamic Earth.

The twentieth century had seen change with supersonic speed. Two World Wars have occurred that century and there is still the constant threat of the Third, and some say Final. The second half of the twentieth century was one of the bloodiest in history. More than 120 wars were fought, killing 25 million and maiming 75 million more. Some call this era the Age of Technology, with the birth of the car, air and space travel, telecommunications and satellite communication, where the advances of the computer can be seen in every area of life. We have witnessed the large-scale exploitation and abuse of natural resources, the exploration and destruction of land, sea and space, and the beginnings of a deeper understanding of our genetic composition. Whilst most of the world's children are dying from hunger and malnutrition everyday, over the past 25 years, the richest fifth of the world's population has seen its share of the planet's wealth grow from 69% to more than 80%, largely through immoral means. We are in exciting and dangerous times. From what history has taught us, the time ahead of us looks similar - keep that which is good for mankind and prevent that which is bad. The state of mankind has always been an issue of debate - now is the time for the talking to stop, and for the action to begin.

Have we, as Muslims, 'progressed', taking the word 'progress' to mean increased qualitatively as measured in our faith (*iman*) and increased quantitatively in terms of the rise in the number of Muslims around the world? The answer is split. We have increased, greater than ever before. But our faith has gone down. Let us look at how us Muslims have improved by looking at events in Mecca and Medina, the centre of Islam.

THE PAST

Mecca and Medina, 1950 -
Only 100,000 performed the Hajj pilgrimage.

THE PRESENT

Mecca and Medina, 2001 -
Around 3,000,000 Muslims gathered in Mecca towards in February 2001 to perform the annual Hajj pilgrimage to Islam's holiest site. Beginning in 1984, King Fahd directed one of the most remarkable construction projects of the 20th century, a major enlargement of the Holy Mosque of Mecca as well as a massive expansion of the Prophet's mosque in the holy city of Medina. The work on Islam's two holiest mosques cost more than $25 billion. In Mecca, a major four-tiered extension more than doubled the available prayer space. In Medina, the area of the mosque was expanded more than 10 times to 165,000 sq m. Both mosques can each accommodate more than 1 million Muslim worshippers. Among the innovations are domes that can open and close depending on the weather, and huge mechanically operated umbrellas that shade the piazza areas from the desert sun. The Medina mosque now has one of the largest, and most technologically advanced air-conditioners in the world.

NUMBERS ARE UP, BUT THERE IS NO JUSTICE

THE FUTURE

A leap from a couple of thousand to many million worshippers at Mecca and Medina is a good start, but what is our real status? Are we sad that there is no Caliphate? Are we ashamed of our lack of unity? Are we sad because around the world Muslims are being persecuted so much and fear that our turn is soon? Are we disgusted that in the lands of the great people of Islam and in Muslim countries around the world, debauchery and decadence is on the increase? Are we enraged at the thought that women and children are raped, murdered and mutilated because they are Muslims? The answers to these questions is a sad yes, and it just contributes to making us more depressed.

Islam FORBIDS depression. The flip-side of the coin is much better - a different perspective.

Islam is the One True Religion and we believe in ALLAH,
HE who has created EVERYTHING.

A totally different ball-game. New Rules, New Attitude, New Future.

What is Islam?

'There is no God but Allah and Muhammad is His Messenger'
Islam is hope, optimism, justice, truth, salvation, happiness, joy, Paradise.

Who are Muslims?

Those who practice the way of life of Islam.

Why is this Millennium so important to Islam?

By the Mercy of Allah, the new Millennium will be the first time Islam is the largest religion on Earth and when it will become THE MOST POWERFUL FORCE ON THIS EARTH.

Why do we need to know this?

So that those of you who SAY you are Muslims should ACT as Muslims -
Islamic Power NEVER Corrupts.

To those who need the warning, the Prophet (pbuh) said:
'Happy is the one who accepts the warning of another.'

To those Non-Muslims, this is The Future and The Truth - embrace it under no compulsion.
Realise with your minds and heart that this is the best and only way of life.

How do we accomplish this?

By the Majesty of Allah, the path will be shown NOW.

'I can only show you the door, YOU have to open it.'

'Allah made it but a Message of Hope for you,
and an assurance to your hearts.
And there is no victory except from
Allah,
the Almighty, the All-Wise.'
(HQ, 3:126)

HOW TO BE A MUSLIM IN THE MILLENNIUM

Being a Muslim in the Millennium is the same it has been throughout time. The mindset is what matters. You are the torchbearers of The Message which the Prophets of Allah have been privileged to be given. It is your mission to spread this Message. You must have the same mindset as Adam, Noah, Abraham, Moses, Jesus and Muhammad (peace be upon all of them), for these were some of the blessed Prophets to have been chosen by Allah to spread His Message. It is your job to continue their job till the Earth becomes the Islamic Earth.

This is what it takes to be a Muslim. (Practising, acting, believing)

You need to know which Path will grant you salvation. Sects are appearing all over the world, claiming to be Muslims, yet are outside the fold of Islam because they do not agree with the fundamentals of the religion and some have been specifically designed to subvert Islam.

One Force

'And hold fast, all of you together, to the Rope of Allah and do not be divided. And remember Allah's Favour upon you, for you were once enemies to one another, but He joined your hearts together, so that by His Grace, you became brothers.' (HQ, 3:103)

'Let there arise from amongst you a group of people inviting to all that is good, enjoining the good and forbidding the evil. Those are the successful ones.' (HQ, 3:104)

'Indeed this Ummah of yours is one Ummah, and I am your Lord, so worship Me alone.' (HQ, 21:92)

'And obey Allah and His Messenger and do not dispute with one another, lest you lose courage and your strength departs, and be patient. Surely, Allah is with those who are patient.' (HQ, 8:46)

The Sects

'Indeed those who divide their religion and break up into sects, you have no concern with them in the least. Their affair is only with Allah who will tell them what they used to do.' (HQ, 6:159)

The Prophet (pbuh) recited this Verse and said: 'These people are those who invent reprehensible things in the concept and practice of religion (*bid'ah*) and the followers of vain desires in this Ummah, and their repentance will not be accepted by Allah.'

'And do not be like those who differed amongst themselves after the clear evidence had come to them: for them is a tremendous punishment.' (HQ, 3:105)

'And this is My Straight Path, so follow it, and do not follow other paths that will separate you from His Path. This he has ordained for you so that you may become righteous and honourable Muslims.' (HQ, 6:153)

By the Grace of Allah, there is one group of Muslims, the main group which will be saved. In Islam, there is ONLY ONE PATH: 'THE STRAIGHT PATH' (HQ, 1:6). THERE ARE AS MANY ROADS TO THE STRAIGHT PATH AS THERE ARE PEOPLE - BUT THERE IS ONLY ONE STRAIGHT PATH. On the Straight Path, there is a huge spectrum of shades, colours and opinions but they all believe in the same virtues, and only differ where they are allowed to differ. There can be no difference in the Holy Qur'an and the Sunnah of the Prophet (pbuh) - these are eternal - however, in matters of individual reasoning (*ijtihad*), of course, there will be differences as there will be similarities. You want to be in this group and on this Path. In fact, at this very point, the vast majority of the Muslims reading this are in that group. However, the vast majority of you Muslims are SITTING on the Path. It is time for you to STAND UP & START MOVING FORWARD. By the Grace of Allah, all Muslims will be progressing on this Path by the time they've finished reading. Welcome on board!

The Promise

'Allah has promised to those amongst you who have faith and righteous deeds that He will certainly grant them the *khilafah* (succession of rule) in the land, as He granted it to those before them and gave them the authority to practice their religion which He has chosen for them.' (HQ, 24:55)

The Prophet (pbuh) said 'Give good tidings to this Ummah about a high position, being established upon the Earth, victory, and a high position in this world and the Hereafter.'

Sincere Advice

'If you differ in anything amongst yourselves then refer it back to **Allah and His Messenger**, if you do truly believe in Allah and the Last Day. That is better and more suitable for final determination.' (HQ, 4:59)

The Prophet (pbuh) said in his Farewell Sermon: 'I am leaving you with what if you hold fast to, you will never go astray: **The Book of Allah the Almighty and the Sunnah of the Prophet** (pbuh).'

The Prophet's advice (pbuh) to Muslims living towards the End of Time was 'Stick to the **main body of the Muslims** and their Imam (leader in prayer).'

The Prophet (pbuh) said:
**'By Him in Whose Hand is my soul,
my Ummah will split into 73 sects:
1 will enter Paradise and 72 will enter Hell.'**
Someone asked, 'O Messenger of Allah, who will they be?'
He replied, **'The main body of the Muslims (*al-Jama'ah*).'**

The main body of the Muslims (*al-Jama'ah as-Sunnah*) means Muslims who follow The Holy Qur'an, the Sunnah of the Prophet (pbuh), authentic jurisprudence and other sciences in all circumstances without introducing any changes or imposing their own confused ideas.

THERE IS NO COMPULSION IN ISLAM

The Prophet (pbuh) was known for making things easy rather than difficult and he always tended towards moderation. He said when instructing people whom he was sending on missions: **'Make matters easy rather than difficult. Show people the bright side of things rather than the hateful ones. Preach in a moderate and direct way.'**

He knew that there were degrees in faith and that religion should be easy on a person and not difficult: **'Religion is very easy and whoever overburdens himself in his religion will not be able to continue in that way. So you should not be extremists,** but try to be near to perfection and receive the good tidings that you will be rewarded; and gain strength by offering prayers in the mornings, afternoons and during the last hours of the night.' The theme was continuous throughout his preaching as he also said **'This religion is lenient, so practice it gently. Do not make the worship of Allah hateful to yourselves.** If you make it onerous you will achieve nothing but strain yourselves.' One day, a new Muslim went to the Prophet (pbuh) and told him that he could not perform all the prayers and wanted to perform one of them, the Prophet (pbuh) did not forbid him and his Companions wondered at that. When the man left, he said to them **'When his faith grows strong he will perform them all.'**

Additionally, the Prophet (pbuh) said **'A strong Muslim is more loved by Allah and dearer to Him than a weak one. But there is good in both.'** So the Prophet's words in praise of strength emphasises that Islam is a religion of varying degrees of faith. Do not go for the extremes, go for balance - and only fulfill your potential.

TO BE A MUSLIM,
YOU MUST BELIEVE, THINK AND PRACTICE THESE WORDS
'THERE IS NO GOD BUT ALLAH, AND MUHAMMAD IS HIS MESSENGER.'

The Prophet (pbuh) said 'Abandon that which gives you doubt for that which gives you no doubt.'

THE FAITH OF ISLAM

Bear witness that there is no god but Allah and Muhammad is His Messenger.

Allah is the One True and Only God.
He is the Supreme Controller and Regulator.

You must believe in all the Messengers of Allah. Allah's guidance to mankind began with Adam (pbuh) and was completed with Muhammad (pbuh). Muhammad (pbuh) is the Seal of the Prophets and there will be no Revelations after him.

You must believe in the angels of Allah
such as Jibril (Gabriel), Mika'il (Michael), 'Izra'il (Azrael) and Israfil (Israphael).

You must believe that the Holy Qur'an is the Final and Complete Revelation of Allah. You must believe in all the revealed books which are mentioned in the Qur'an. They are the *Zabur* of Dawud (Psalms of David), *Tawrat* of Musa (Torah of Moses), *Injil* of Isa (Gospel of Jesus) and the Holy Qur'an revealed to Muhammad (pbuh). Of the Divine Books, only the Holy Qur'an exists in its original form, unchanged and unmixed.

You must believe in the Day of Judgment (*Yamuddin*)

You must believe that you will die
and that you will be resurrected by the Will of Allah in the Eternal Hereafter (*Akhirah*)

The statement, called the Faith in Detail, *Al-Imanul Mufassil*:

'I believe in Allah, in His angels, in His books, in His messengers, in the Last Day (Day of Judgment) and in the fact that everything good and bad is decided by Allah, the Almighty, and in the Life after Death.'

THE FIVE PILLARS - A FIST

Look at your hand.
You have five fingers.
Clench your hand into a fist.
Which is stronger? The fist.

Each finger represents one of the Pillars of Islam.
The clenched fist represents the Muslim who is performing his five basic duties of Islam.
He is strong and resilient compared
to the Muslim who only performs one of the prescribed duties.

This is where your future lies.
Perform the five basic duties of Islam and everything else will flow from there.
Do them in earnest and effectively and only then will they have any significant effect.
'And We shall make easy for you the easy Way.' (HQ, 87:8)

THE PILLARS OF ISLAM

THE DECLARATION OF FAITH - *SHAHADAH*

'I bear witness that there is no God but Allah and that Muhammad is the Messenger of Allah.'

5 COMPULSORY DAILY WORSHIPS TO ALLAH - *SALAH*

The most important duty of a Muslim. Allah has created us to worship Him. He says in the Holy Qur'an: 'I have not created jinn and mankind for any other purpose except to worship Me.' (HQ, 51:56).

COMPULSORY WELFARE CONTRIBUTION - *ZAKAH*

'Those who establish regular worship and pay Zakat and believe in Allah and in the Last Day:
To them shall We give a great reward.'
(HQ, 4:162)

(Set at 2.5% per year on everything you own.)

FASTING IN RAMADAN = *SAWM*

'O you who believe! Fasting is prescribed for you as it was prescribed to those before you,
that you may become righteous and honourable Muslims.'
(HQ, 2:183)

Prescribed on all adult Muslims from dawn to sunset everyday of Ramadan,
the ninth month of the Islamic calendar.

THE PILGRIMAGE TO MECCA - *HAJJ*

'Pilgrimage to Mecca is a duty men owe to Allah - those who can afford the journey.'
(HQ, 3:97)

The pilgrimage to the Ka'aba, the House of Allah at Mecca, is prescribed on those Muslims in the month of Dhul' Hijjah, the 12th Islamic month for those who can afford to make the journey at least once in their lifetime.

These five duties equal **JIHAD** = STRIVING HARD IN THE CAUSE OF ALLAH

'Those who believed, and emigrated and strove hard and fought in Allah's Cause,
with their wealth and their lives, have the highest rank in the sight of Allah:
Those are the successful.' (HQ, 9:20)

The use of all our energies and resources to establish the Islamic system in life, in order to gain Allah's Pleasure.

A Muslim's duty is obedience and submission (*Islam*) to the Will of Allah. However, you cannot submit passively or simply accept this set of duties as rituals -
YOU MUST IMPOSE ALLAH'S WILL IN HISTORY.

You need to become representatives of Allah's Word on this Earth and you have to perform your duties purely to please Him:

**'It is He Who has made you the Agents of the Earth:
And He has raised you in ranks, some above others so
that He may try you in the gifts He has given you.
Surely, your Lord is quick in punishment and certainly He is Oft-Forgiving, Most Merciful.' (HQ, 6:165)**

Muslims, even if you work with your hands in the fields of Bangladesh under the blazing heat of the sun or are a businessman lodged on the top floor of a skyscraper in Malaysia- you have all entered into a DIVINE CONTRACT, A DIVINE TRUST, the *Amanah* with Allah.

'Truly, We did offer The Trust to the heavens and the earth and the mountains.'
(HQ, 33:72)

Indicator of success: Faith in Allah and Righteous Actions -

'(It will be said to him:) "Read your (own) record:
sufficient is your soul this Day to make out an account against you."'
(HQ, 17:14)

You fail to please Allah:
The Blazing Fire of Hell.

'Verily, the tree of Zaqqum will be the food of the sinful.
Like molten brass it will boil in their insides -
like the boiling of scalding water.'
(HQ, 44:43-46)

You succeed in pleasing Allah:
The Blissful Gardens of Paradise.

'Truly Allah will admit those who believe (in the Oneness of Allah) and do righteous good deeds,
to Gardens under which rivers flow where they will be adorned with
bracelets of gold and pearls and their garments will be of silk.'
(HQ, 22:23)

CHOOSE

'Verily, Allah has purchased the lives of the believers, their lives and their properties
for the price that theirs shall be Paradise.'
(HQ, 9:111)

'Then Allah misleads whom He wills, and guides whom He wills.
And He is the Almighty, The All-Wise.' (HQ, 14:4)

THE PERFECTION OF ISLAM

Archangel Jibril asked 'What is the perfection of Islam?'
Allah's Messenger (pbuh) replied
'To worship Allah as if you see Him,
and if you cannot achieve this state of devotion,
then you must consider that He can see you.'

YOUR REWARD : THE PATH TO PARADISE

Your reward for pleasing your Creator in this life is going to Paradise.
Paradise is a Destination and The Straight Path is the Map

DESTINATON PARADISE

**'Verily, the dwellers of Paradise that Day, will be busy with joyful things.
They and their wives will be in pleasant shade, reclining on thrones.
They will have therein fruits (of all kinds), and all that they ask for.
It will be said to them: "Peace be upon you, a Word from the Lord, Most Merciful."'**
(HQ, 36:55-58)

The mind cannot imagine this place. Its gardens have rivers flowing under them, and is filled with palaces built of gold and silver bricks. Its earth is perfumed with the scent of musk *Al-Adhfar* (an outstandingly beautiful smell), the scattered pebbles are pearls and sapphire. Even its dust is of saffron, whilst the tents of Paradise are of hollow pearls. There are the fruits of the sweetest taste, all of those of this earth and also many of those not of the earth. Residing in the Garden are the blessed believers of Allah who eat as much as they like and remain in the best of health, do not excrete, nor urinate, and even their sweat smells of sweet musk. A place of such bliss that it is filled with merriment and where the blessed drink celestial wine, which does not dumb the senses or make one immoral. They will stay here and enjoy themselves forever. The screen of Paradise will be raised and the successful ones will look at The Face of Allah. An infinite sense of love and peace. Prophet Muhammad (pbuh) gave us the joyous news, and he was a human like you and me, yet the Best Example of Mankind.

**'Allah has promised to the believers - men and women -
Gardens under which rivers flow to dwell therein forever and beautiful mansions in Gardens of 'Adn.
But the greatest pleasure is the Good Pleasure of Allah. THAT is the supreme success!'** (HQ, 9:72)

They chose LIFE, they chose ISLAM.

THE BEST OF PARADISE: *AL-FIRDAUS*

The Prophet (pbuh) said: 'Whosoever believes in Allah and His Messenger (pbuh) offers prayer perfectly and fasts in the month of Ramadan, will rightfully be granted Paradise by Allah, no matter whether he fights in Allah's cause or remains in the land he was born in.' Then people said, 'O Allah's Messenger! Shall we inform the people of this great news?' He said: 'Paradise has one-hundred grades which Allah has prepared for those who perform Jihad in His cause, and the distance between each of the two levels are like the distance between the Heavens and the Earth. **So, when you ask Allah (for something), ask for *Al-Firdaus* which is the best and highest part of Paradise.'**

APPEARANCE IN PARADISE

The Prophet (pbuh) said:
'The inhabitants of Paradise will enter Paradise hairless, beardless and as if their eyes are anointed with kohl, and they will be aged thirty or thirty-three years.'

SEXUAL PROWESS IN PARADISE

The Prophet of Allah (pbuh) said:
'The believers in Paradise will be given the strength of so and so for sexual intercourse.'
It was said to him: 'O Messenger of Allah, will he be capable of that?'
He said: **'He will be given the strength of a hundred (i.e. men).'**

THE WOMEN OF PARADISE

**'And we shall marry them to *Hur'ayn* - stunningly beautiful women
with intense black irises of the eyes and intense white sceleras.'** (HQ, 52:20)
'The *Qasirat ut-Tur*f - chaste female wives desiring none except their husbands - with whom no man or jinn has had sexual intercourse with before. In beauty they are like rubies and coral.' (HQ, 55:55-56)

THE MAP : THE STRAIGHT PATH (The Right)

FAITH

The statement, called the Faith in Detail, *Al-Imanul Mufassil*:
'I believe in Allah, in His angels, in His books, in His messengers, in the Last Day (Day of Judgment) and in the fact that everything good and bad is decided by Allah, the Almighty, and in the Life after Death.'

RIGHTEOUS DEEDS

THE DECLARATION OF FAITH - *SHAHADAH'*

'I bear witness that there is no God but Allah and that Muhammad is the Messenger of Allah.'

5 COMPULSORY DAILY WORSHIPS TO ALLAH - *SALAH*

The most important duty of a Muslim. Allah has created us to worship Him.

COMPULSORY WELFARE CONTRIBUTION - *ZAKAH*

(Set at 2.5% per year on everything you own.)

FASTING IN RAMADAN = *SAWM*

Prescribed on all adult Muslims from dawn to sunset everyday of Ramadan, the ninth month of the Islamic calendar.

THE PILGRIMAGE TO MECCA - *HAJJ*

The pilgrimage to the Ka'aba, the House of Allah at Mecca, in Dh'ul Hijjah, prescribed on those Muslims who can afford to make the journey at least once in their lifetime.

These five duties equal **JIHAD = STRUGGLE IN THE NAME OF ALLAH**
The use of all our energies and resources to establish the Islamic system in life, in order to gain Allah's Favour.

THESE ARE VIRTUES A MUSLIM MUST POSSESS:

Kindness, Honesty, Truthfulness, Perseverance, Tolerance, Firmness against odds and evil, Punctuality, Courage, Trustworthiness, Justice, Chastity, Hard work, Generosity, Forgiveness, Reliance on Allah, Good Intentions and Good actions, Politeness, Modesty, Brotherhood, Contentment, Learning, Thankfulness, Steadfastness, Sincere Repentance, Giving and Accepting Gifts, Visiting the Sick

BE KIND TO YOUR PARENTS

'Thank Me as well as your parents: Unto Me is the Final Destination.' (HQ, 31:14)
'And serve them with tenderness and humility and say:
"My Lord, have mercy on them, just as they cared for me as a little child."' (HQ, 17:23-24)

BE KIND TO THE NEEDY

'And (show) kindness to (your) parents and to near relatives, orphans, the needy and to the neighbour who is your relative and the neighbour who is not your relative.' (HQ, 4:36)

BE KIND TO ORPHANS

'The orphan must not be oppressed.' (HQ, 93:9)
'Those who live unjustly on orphan's property only suck up fire into their bellies, and they will be burnt in the Blazing Fire.' (HQ, 4:10)

BE KIND TO MUSLIMS

Practice the unity of Islam through right intentions, words and actions with each other.

KEEP PROMISES

'Fulfill your promise, for every promise will be inquired into.' (HQ, 17:34)

BE JUST

Be just in our thoughts, actions and decisions, for justice is in every element of Islam.

THE MAP : THE STRAIGHT PATH (The Wrong)

THE ASSOCIATION OF PARTNERS WITH ALLAH = *SHIRK*

ONLY ALLAH IS WORTHY OF OUR WORSHIP AND HELP US

He Alone is The One who we can ask for help and He Alone can provide this aid.

ONLY ALLAH HAS KNOWLEDGE OF THE UNSEEN

We must not believe in what the soothsayers, fortune-tellers or astrologers inform us with.

THE ONLY LAW TO BE OBEYED IS ALLAH'S LAW

We must obey Allah only. Nothing can come between us and the obedience of Allah.
We must obey what Allah has made lawful and shun what He has made forbidden.

SINS

THESE ARE THE QUALITIES A MUSLIM MUST AVOID

Lying, Back-biting, Spying, Jealousy, Anger, Pride, Abuse, Taunting, Suspicion, Fraud, Extravagance, Arrogance, Hoarding, Mischief, Corruption, Mockery, Ridicule and Hypocrisy.

PROTECT OUR MINDS

We must not think of evil thoughts which will harm us, and cause our morality to be corrupted

PROTECT OUR EARS

We must avoid futile talk, filled with sin or obscenity, lies, sexual music, slander, defamation, blasphemy and talks that separate us from our loved ones or talks of disbelief.

PROTECT OUR EYES

We must lower our gaze at that which Allah has forbidden to us, such as a woman/man who it is lawful for us to marry, a Muslim or a disbeliever, whether they are virtuous or an adulterer.

PROTECT OUR TONGUES

We must not speak of abhorrence, obscenity, inequity, evil, lies, falsehood, slander, backbiting or defamation, curse or revile anyone.

PROTECT OUR STOMACHS

We must not eat unlawful food or drink - nor must we eat from usury, carrion, swine, nor drink intoxicants, smoke tobacco or other intoxicants (i.e. drugs)

PROTECT OUR PRIVATE PARTS

We must not have sexual intercourse with others than our wife(s)/husband in Islam, or that which our right hand possesses, from what Allah has allowed and made lawful to us.

PROTECT OUR HANDS

We must not harm anyone by striking or killing them, nor must we steal, gamble, or indulge in corruption.

PROTECT OUR LEGS

We must not approach temptations, immoralities, evil or matters that do not concern us.

PROTECT OUR OATHS, WITNESSES & TRUSTS

We must not breach our promises knowingly. We must not exceed our agreement, testify to falsehood nor must we betray our trusts.

PROTECT OUR WEALTH

We must not squander our wealth, be extravagant with it, neglect it or spend it uselessly, or leave it without advancing or improving it.

PROTECT OUR FAMILIES & CHILDREN

In regards to their thinking, their manners and their beliefs, we must ward off from them which is harmful, damaging or that which may corrupt their souls or their minds.

THE GUARANTEE

YOU ARE THE AGENTS OF ALLAH (*KHALIFAH*)

Men and women who believe in Allah are His agents on earth.
Creation and all that it contains is a sacred trust from Allah and not the property of any individual, group or generation. We are responsible for maintaining and preserving the integrity of Allah's creation - the Earth, the environment, the flora and fauna.
We will be held accountable for our use and Allah forbids our abuse of this trust in this world and the Hereafter.

YOU WILL ACQUIRE KNOWLEDGE (*'ILM*)

You are obliged to gain knowledge.
A Muslim society can only be just when it is a knowledge-based society.
Muslim communities have to ensure that experts in every branch of knowledge - commerce, law, medicine, education - are adequately represented in the community.
The expert in a particular field is called an *alim.*
A religious scholar, a lawyer, a physicist, a philosopher, a merchant banker- are all known as *ulema.*
You must acquire knowledge only with the aim of promoting beauty and dignity, freedom and justice.
You can only acquire knowledge through just means.

YOU WILL ESTABLISH JUSTICE ON THIS EARTH (*ADL*)

Justice is a supreme value.
You cannot be just unless you have knowledge.
You are here to establish justice on earth.
All believers must behave towards one another in a just way.

YOURSELF: Justice begins with oneself, and involves fulfilling the needs of one's body, mind and spirit.
FAMILY: Be affectionate, honest and loyal towards your spouse
Show equal love and affection towards all your children
Respect towards one's parents and elders
COMMUNAL: It is your duty, as a Muslim to stand up against all kinds of oppression, even if this involves your relations, society or country.

This is the complete path, but we must prepare to benefit from this by applying it into our lives, and this will not be possible except with correct authentic knowledge, which is built upon the Holy Book of Allah and the Sunnah of His Messenger (pbuh). This proverb from Muslims in Arabia is worth heeding, 'If God did not forgive, Paradise would be empty.'

ALWAYS REMEMBER THAT ALLAH IS THE MOST COMPASSIONATE, THE MOST MERCIFUL

'Verily, Allah forgives not that partners should be set up with Him, but He forgives except that to whom He wills; and whoever sets up partners with Allah in worship, he has indeed invented a tremendous sin.'
(HQ, 4:48)

'If you are grateful, I will give you more.' (HQ, 14:7)

'Is there any reward for good other than good?' (HQ, 55:60)

The Prophet (pbuh) said 'Whoever makes it easy for someone in difficulty,
Allah will make it easy for him in the world and the Next Life.'

'This day I have perfected your religion for you for you, completed My Favour upon you and have chosen for you Islam as your religion.' (HQ, 5:3)

The End of the World? SUPREME ISLAM

Everyone around the world fears that the world may come to an end. They feel it. They know it is uncertain. The world cannot end until Islam is supreme on this Earth once more. Now is the time for Islam.

GLOBAL ISLAMIC BIODATA

Population
Millennium Total: 1..5 billion
World Population: 6.0 billion

1in 4 people on Earth is a MUSLIM

60 sovereign states in various states of development, incorporating more than 60 languages with various backgrounds, classes, colours, styles, clothes, customs, appearances, greetings but ONE MESSAGE.

Landmass 31,414,544 sq. km

¼ of the total global surface.

Resources
50% of world raw materials.
82% of the world's oil.
60% of the total mineral resources of the world
- oil, gas, gold, silver, copper, zinc, uranium, etc.
70% of the world's rubber.
75% of the world's jute.
40% of the world's cotton.
67% of the world's spices.

Health
60% Access to Clean Water
60% Access to Health Services

Literacy
61% Total Literacy, Adult Males 70%, Adult Females 52%
Primary pupil to Teacher Ratio 50:1

Trade
Total Global Export US $272 billion
Total Global Imports US $283 billion

Debt US $706 billion

We have all these resources in our lands, but we lack health, literacy, and the ability to live under the Laws of Allah.

These statistics show that the Kingdom of Allah, the unification of the Islamic World in all spheres of life, is coming.

The Archangel Jibril came to the Prophet (pbuh) asking when the Day of Judgment would come, and he only replied, 'The one questioned knows no more of it that the questioner.' But as the Holy Qur'an states:

'They ask you about the Hour: "When will be the appointed time?" Say: "The knowledge thereof is with my Lord. None can reveal its time but He. Heavy is the burden through the heaven and Earth. It shall not come upon you except all of a sudden."' (HQ, 7:187)

HE IS COMING, BUT ALLAH KNOWS WHEN

Apocalyptic expectations are not new in Islamic history: they appeared, for instance, in connection with the Islamic millennium. Imam al-Suyuti, the greatest scholar of mediaeval Egypt, was concerned about the nervous expectation many Muslims had about the year 1000 AH. Would it herald the end of the world as many thought?

Imam al-Suyuti allayed these fears by examining all the hadiths he could find about the lifetime of this Ummah. He wrote a short book which he called 'Proof that this Ummah will survive the Millennium' - he concluded that there was no evidence that the first Millennium of Islam would herald the end of human history. But in words which will awaken our generation, he speculated that the hadiths at his disposal indicated that the signs which will usher in the Mahdi, the Guided Leader, the return of the Prophet Jesus (pbuh) and the Anti-Christ (*al-Massih al-Dajjal*) are most likely to appear in the **FIFTEENTH ISLAMIC CENTURY; IN OTHER WORDS, OUR CENTURY.**

But all these well-founded speculations and extrapolations were submissive to the Imam's deep Islamic awareness that knowledge of the future is with Allah; and only Prophets can prophesy.

'Verily, His Command, when he intends a thing, is only that He says to it, "Be!" and it is!' (HQ, 36:82)

The West believes that it is the most dominant culture and civilisation that this Earth knows and will ever know. Indeed, the concepts and attributes that have shaped Western culture have successfully been exported to every corner of the Earth. After the collapse of communism in 1991, Francis Fukuyama, head of the Policy Planning staff of the American State Department in 1991, published his article (and later his book) proclaiming 'The End of History.' The Western way of life would impose itself globally and that there are no other ideologies which could compete with these attributes of rationalism, liberalism, individualism, tolerance, parliament and human rights. These are the attributes which are seen by Western academics at large as being those of the 'ideal' society.

The West believes that its role forever lies at being the righteous judge, jury and executioner of international policy for the immediate and long-term future. The way that it has gained this role is through the successful export of this brand of ideology to other parts of the world; 'The Third World', 'The Islamic World', 'The Poor World', the submissive and passive parts of the world.

'And those who came before you: they were mightier than you in power, and more abundant in wealth and children. They had enjoyed their portion: and you have yours, as did those before you; and you indulge in idle talk as they did. Their work in this world and in the Hereafter is worthless. And they are the losers.' (HQ, 9:69)

Anyone who has interacted with the West will soon realise that the values of rationalism, liberalism, individualism, tolerance, parliament and human rights are empty buzzwords. They are to be used when you want to promote your own interests, and these notions are only worth something if they comply with your personal agenda or the agenda of your financial supporters. Indeed, students of politics and modern history soon realise that the West has only one real principle: opportunism for self-interest. True, there is style, but style never lasts when there is no Divine Substance.

**'How many generations before them did We destroy?
In the end, they cried for mercy, when there was no longer time for being saved!' (HQ, 38:3)**

THE BEST OF MANKIND

The West today is built on the achievements of the Islamic world's past in nearly every way - politically, economically, artistically, scientifically and more. Today, when so many Muslim students flock to Western universities to learn, the situation four centuries ago was reversed whereby our friends in the West were coming over to study with us and to understand how we had become the most prosperous region on Earth. They wanted to know what the key to this success was: Knowledge (*'ILM*)

HOW TO BE THE BEST OF MANKIND : THE PURSUIT OF KNOWLEDGE

Early Muslim societies knew from the Holy Qur'an and Prophet Muhammad (pbuh) that the only way that they would have a just society was if it was a knowledge-based society. Without knowledge, you cannot be just. Much in the same way that a lack of evidence in a court of law means that it makes the decision of the court more difficult to determine a verdict. Therefore, the Qur'anic emphasis on knowledge became the main driving seat of the Islamic world. The desire 'to know' transformed Islam into a world civilisation. Initially, with the focus that the Muslims were the representatives of Allah on Earth, the Muslims began to translate and absorb knowledge from other civilisations, including Egypt, Babylonia, Greece, India, China and Persia.

Within a short period, books from Greek, Syriac, Sanskrit, Chinese and Persian were translated into Arabic - one of the greatest cultural transmissions in human history. After translation came the long and arduous task of critically sifting, analysing and accepting or rejecting the learning of other civilisations. This is when the entire Muslim civilisation became engulfed in intense debate - and the book became the key vehicle for communication of ideas. In every field imaginable, the Muslims were the best on this Earth from the seventh century to the fourteenth century in the pursuit of knowledge.

HOW THE MUSLIMS DECLINED : THEY STOPPED THE PURSUIT OF KNOWLEDGE

As Muslims stopped pursuing knowledge which Allah had made obligatory for them to do so, the Islamic world became more and more unjust. Today, there is a lack of justice in the majority of the Islamic world.

In the absence of new ideas, reflection and understanding of changing circumstances which would have occurred through the pursuit of knowledge, the Islamic world lost its dynamism and degenerated. Today, there is a lack of dynamism in the Islamic world.

HOW THE WEST BECAME THE DOMINANT CULTURE

Up to the 16th century, the flow of knowledge was strictly from Islam to Europe. The works of Muslim scholars were regularly translated into Latin, and other European languages, used as text books and practical manuals. European scholars and thinkers were regular visitors at Islamic centres of learning. European students went to Cordoba Fez, Cairo, Baghdad, Samarkhand and Bukhara to study under the great masters just as Muslim students in the present day come to the West for further study. Arabic was the language of science and culture, and those who cared for thought and learning showed their concern by dressing like Muslim scholars.

The European Renaissance and all the progress in science, technology, medicine, learning, and humanism that it produced, was built squarely on the shoulders of Muslim scholars and thinkers. Indeed, the Renaissance is inconceivable without the contribution of Muslim civilisation. The achievements of Muslim scholars and scientists were frequently plagiarised, deliberately and systematically downgraded, undermined and brushed aside. It is only at the present time that the truth is coming out.

The West grew strong on the secondary and tertiary principles of Islam; those of hard work, enjoining the right, forbidding the wrong, taking care of the poor through social services and more. A glance through the modern history of the West and its formation will quickly make one realise that the West used the principle of Islam to gain its present position of dominance, a cunning and remarkable feat. Indeed, one recalls social justice being introduced in the United Kingdom by the Liberal Party in the 1800s, making it a political brand name, a feat which Islam had already accomplished more than twelve centuries ago. Prohibition in the USA is another example, whereby the Government knew that alcohol consumption would eventually drive down their populations in term of lifestyle and health, a fact confirmed by the sad rapid obesity of many Americans today. Additionally, when the Americans entered Saudi Arabia as part of the oil company, ARAMCO, many Americans worked with the determination and hard work that characterises Islam.

In contrast, the Islamic world talked about Allah but did not do His work effectively. The West used His principles to become the dominant force, to show Muslims that when you turn away from the Laws of Allah, He will favour another nation over you. The West realises that it was built on the secondary principles of Islam: the primary principle of Islam is the Sovereignty of Allah on this Earth. It is largely missing this Divine inspiration, and the West has now realised that the game is up:

Islam has to become the dominant force on this Earth.

Islam the religion which the simpleton and intellectual both can adhere to is today far different from its adherents, the Muslims. The Islamic World (*Dar al-Islam*), where Allah's word is Law, today does not exist along national or regional lines. The Earth is filled with injustice. It is true that there are countries where the awe-inspiring beauty of dozens of muezzins' voices calling the faithful to prayer can be heard across vast city-landscapes. But in the streets and homes, debauchery and decadence have spread and are spreading fast. Whilst importing the technological advances of the West, the Islamic world has also adopted the debaucherous and decadent lifestyle, in their homes, if not in public. A Western tourist who may have seen the beauty of a Muslim in *Salah*, when visiting the Islamic world, can in many of these so-called Muslim countries find alcohol, pork, pornography, the pursuit of wealth placed above all else. Everything wrong and more is available in the Islamic world, and it is just a question for finding the market and paying the price.

Countering this, there is an invisible force = True Islam. It is scattered in some homes, mosques, small regions of the world, Muslim organisations, and is increasing at an unpredictably fast rate. The progress of this invisible force is so unpredictable and rapid that even the fastest computers and satellites cannot gain an accurate focus on the situation. That is why it can be firmly predicted with the Grace of Allah, that the Islamic world will consume and spread justice everywhere in the Millennium, through the efforts of Muslims.

Remember that the West largely believes in one concept: self-interest. It is up to us to know what our own interests are, know what the West's are, and then see which match and which do not. In academic circles and foreign policy, Islam as a phenomenon is taken very seriously, often perceived as a threat, a trembling force, an invisible force, an unpredictable force, and most dangerous of all, a Divinely-inspired force. Governments, academics and the media in the West all agree on this perspective: Islam is the new force of the future. A public admission of this is not necessary, but intelligence agencies in the West have as their Number One Focus: Islam.

It is important for Muslims to know the types of people that make up this world. There are more types than those will be mentioned, but these are the ones who are involved directly in Islam in the Millennium.

THE CURRENT PLAYERS

THE TRUE MUSLIMS - THE BEST OF MANKIND

The unified group which is going to play a significant role in Millennium Islam are the Western-standard educated Muslims who are striving to be the Best of Mankind and the Righteous Muslims of the Islamic world, both working in harmony for the glory of Islam. One has been brought up in the dominant culture and is Muslim the other has been brought up in the attacked Islamic culture, and is still Muslim. The Western-born Muslim has visited the Islamic world and through mutual efforts with Muslims based there formulated policies to help revive Islam, the religion. They are co-operating with each other, and are at the cutting edge of life, equipped with the latest technology, best education and skills and will be rewarded in the Hereafter *inshallah*. They are using these attributes to revive Islam for the Millennium and beyond. It is the same Islam, the same Straight Path, that Adam, Noah, Moses, Jesus and Muhammad (peace be upon all of them) but it is just in another time - NOW.

Western-educated Muslims are returning to the Islamic world, as the elite of the country, often as the rulers, sometimes with Islam and at other times without. It is difficult for Muslims to abandon the western ideas and approaches which are in their life, often at the expense of Islam because of such a long-term detachment with Islam. The solution is knowing the benefits of Western culture such as the technology and management training but also the harmful effects such as materialism and lack of morality. To know the good, one must know Islam. Those Muslims who 'study' and practice Islam in their lives and have lived in both spheres can hope to bring the most significant benefits to the world.

They act, whilst others talk. They speak only the right, or do not speak at all. They forbid the wrong, and enjoin the right. These are the believers who are preparing the way for the Leader of Islam in the Millennium, the Mahdi. They fear Allah alone. They are not those men and women of foolish dreams who contend in sects and voice their zeal, 'each party exulting in what it has' (HQ, 23:53).

They are working across international borders, fearing only Allah and utilising all their efforts for the glory of Islam. They are succeeding, and know that they will succeed in the end. They know that Islam in the Millennium is the most powerful force on Earth, and are making the necessary preparations for the arrival of the Guided Leader, the Mahdi, by encouraging the practice of the religion Islam around the globe.

A very small amount of this group, the elite Muslims, interact with the two most important groups to bring about this change:

1) NATIVE WESTERN ELITES

They are often comprised of a variety of religious adherents, rarely Islam. They play a significant role in dictating world affairs and policy. They interact with the enemies of Islam, but most do not know who the enemies of Islam are. They know of Islam only as a phenomenon or threat. They believe that the existence of God and its debate is the highest intellectual point of discourse. They have rarely experienced an active invitation to Islam but are very interested in Islam. They admire Islam from afar, and are beginning to interact with it, and are embracing it rapidly. Many will convert to Islam and help the Muslims.

2) THE MUSLIM MASSES OF THE ISLAMIC WORLD

They are blessed they are able to perform their Islamic duties, lead simple lives and work hard to make a decent living to support their families. Generally, they are good, decent people. A wise Muslim said that it is the humanity of humans that makes them different to all other creation. These people are often abused by leaders who occupy positions and govern them tyrannically, squander the wealth of the economy and force the masses into debt. The masses cry out that they are helpless. As long as they hold tight to the rope of Islam and are not divided, they know that Allah has sent His Army of the Righteous to spread justice over this Earth. Allah is the source of all morality.

Read Le Gai Eaton's account of one of the Muslims - he is not a stereotype, but he does share these beliefs:

'Poor Mustapha does not know much about imperialism, but then he is free from the complexes and inner torments which afflict his more educated brothers. No doubt he could be described as feckless; **but 'Mustapha' is one of 'the people' (in whose name that slogans are coined) and, throughout Islamic history, while rulers have murdered each other, while doctors of law and theology have argued, and while reformers have reformed, the people have gone their way and taken little note of what the great men thought or did**. It may even be that 'Mustapha' and his friends will outlive the great men; the Prophet, curiously enough, seems to have had a few 'Mustaphas' around hum, whom he treated with an amused kindness and tolerance, which has not always been imitated by the religious authorities of later times. Mustapha is not what would usually be called a 'religious person', but however feckless he may be and however negligent with regard to the social obligations imposed by Islam, **he lives and breathes in a religious Universe and understands no other way of life. To suggest to him that there is no God, no divine plan, no after-life, would be like suggesting to a modern Westerner that the Earth is flat and the moon is made of cheese.** One does not give serious consideration to absurdities. **Mustapha is Muslim in that he knows who he is, where he is and to what end he is travelling on his brief earthly journey.**'

THE FUTURE PLAYERS

1) NON-MUSLIMS

The Prophet (pbuh) said 'Islam annihilates all sins that a person committed before embracing Islam.'

a) Those who believe in a Creator, who follow other religions which have grains of Truth in them, but all originated from Allah. You will convert to Islam through the beauty of this religion and the action of some of its righteous people. There is no compulsion in Islam, but the bottom line is whether a God exists or not. If He exists, and He does, then who knows who He really is. Islam answers that question.

b) Those who do not believe in the Creator, but are searching for Answers. 'This can't be all there is to life - there must be more.' Islam is that More. Each day you do not know the reason why you were created is another futile day in your life. Realise that there is no Big Bang theory, and there has to be a Creator. Then discover the Truth.

2) MUSLIMS

a) In Western societies, at the bottom of those societies in term of education and lifestyle and involved in crime must see that Islam will give them the prosperity that they desire.

b) Those who have been deceived and should be advised on how to revert to the One True Path.

c) Those in sects - only unity will be tolerated and there will only be One Ummah of Muslims. There is Only One Path of Truth and you will must abide by the Holy Qur'an and the Sunnah of the Prophet (pbuh)..

d) Secular, weak Muslims who mimic the West in lifestyle, sometimes even Western-educated, are active in the corruption of politics of the Islamic world, made their wealth in an unlawful fashion and cheat their fellow poor Muslims. These are the secular elites of the Islamic world. (However, even in these elites, you will find those Muslims who believe that Islam is the best system of life, but do not speak in fear of mockery or being accused of madness. They work secretly for the glory of Islam) The secular elites of the Islamic world know who they are and must change. They have talents from Allah, and must use their talents not for their selfish ends, but to establish the Kingdom of Allah:

The Messenger of Allah (pbuh) said 'O people! Those who have accepted Islam by their tongues only and Islam has not gone deep into their hearts, do not hurt the Muslims, not taunt them, nor search for their faults. Who so exposes the faults of his Muslim brother, Allah will expose him.
If Allah intends to expose the faults of anyone, surely He will defame such a person, even though he may be in his home.'

However, as Fukuyama believes, we are in the last stage of history, the renewal before the decay. But unlike Fukuyama, there is a stage which he does not realise will come; the time when Islam will reign supreme. Some astute thinkers in the West realise that life is not as rosy as many proclaim. When people have no religion, they do not believe in nothing. They believe in anything. Parvez Mansoor has stated that 'Atheism is taking its toll on the western psyche.' When people believe in anything, the concept of God, a Creator, Higher Being, can be seen as an attractive alternative. Invite all those who are lost and searching for answers, in our case, the Answer, to Islam but first believe, study and practice True Islam first.

We must demand our God-given right to PRACTICE our religion. We need to be the best in terms of education, communications, information technology, health, law, economy, agriculture, entertainment - everything.

Regarding the achievements of Muslims around the globe, Imam W. Deen Muhammad said:

'The more you achieve, the more strength you will have and the more willingness you have to sacrifice and overcome trouble. People are going to envy what you get. When you don't have anything, nobody bothers you. And you are not important enough for the devil to talk to directly. The devil bothers you with the burden that is on you. The more you get, the more you will be envied and the more people will try to take what you have created and produced and carry it to their vaults. If they can't do that, then they want to destroy what you have established.'

How do we do this? **BE** MUSLIMS.

THE SOLUTION TO EVERY PROBLEM = **ISLAM**

The answer lies in the discourse between the Prophet (pbuh)
and Muadh ibn Jabal (may Allah be pleased with him) on his way to al-Yaman as judge.

The Prophet (pbuh): 'How will you decide a problem?'
Muadh : '**According to the Qur'an**.'
The Prophet (pbuh): 'If is not in it?'
Muadh: '**According to the Sunnah**.'
The Prophet (pbuh): 'If it is not in that either?'
Muadh: '**Then I will use my own reasoning**.'

This is the time for ACTION - THE ACTIONS OF THE RIGHTEOUS
You have to believe in Islam -you must be Muslims by NATURE and not just by NAME. You must UNITE.

'The disbelievers are allies to each other. Unless you do what Allah has commanded, there will be a great oppression on Earth and great tyranny.' (HQ, 8: 73)

Unless you become Muslims and unite, this oppression will continue.
Muslims must become Muslims by CONVICTION. Believe in the concept of Allah, He who controls everything. Fear nothing but Him. JUST DO IT.

'If Allah helps you, none can overcome you, but if He foresakes you,
who is there to help you after that? So in Allah then, let the believers put their trust.'
(HQ, 3:160)

PERFORM
MISSION ISLAM

The Islamic Missions will change the face of the world forever, as they will seek to bring unity to the Islamic world. They cannot be considered illegal under international law because they return to the natural concept of providing the basic necessities for humanity's survival.

MI1) The Islamic Relief Network - "Water is Life" seeks to increase the access of water and basic health facilities in the Islamic world from 60% to 100% : **'We made from water every living thing.' (HQ, 21:30)**

MI2) The Islamic Commercial Network - "The Bounty of Allah" seeks the establishment of a global commercial system unifying the Islamic world's resources whereby Muslims trade justly with one another : **'In the Bounty of Allah, and in His Mercy - in that, let them rejoice.' (HQ, 10:58)**

M13) The Islamic Financial Network - 'War on Usury" seeks to eliminate the Islamic world's debt through the establishment of a global financial and banking system based on Islamic law : **'O you who believe! Fear Allah and eliminate usury if you are really believers. And if you do not, then take notice of a war from Allah and His Messenger.' (HQ, 2:278-9)**

MI4) The Islamic Literacy Network - "Read!" seeks to increase the Islamic world's literacy rate from 61% to 100% : **'Read! In the Name of your Lord Who has created.' (HQ, 96:1)**

M15) The Islamic Linguistic Network - "Signs in Languages" seeks to have the Invitation to Islam in every language and for the world to understand the Holy Qur'an in their native language and in Arabic : **'And among His signs are the creation of the heavens and the earth and the differences of your languages and colours. Verily, in that are indeed signs for men of sound knowledge.' (HQ, 30:22)**

MI6) The Islamic Generations Network - "Generation Islam" seeks to increase the youth in the Islamic world's commitment to Islam through Mission Islam across the generations : **'If only they had been of the generations before you who had wisdom, who prohibited men from mischief in the Earth.' (HQ, 11:116)**

M17) The Islamic Global Network - "Planet Islam" seeks to promote True Islam to 4.5 billion people on this Earth in the most suitable manner : **'Say: "This is My Way: I invite unto Allah with sound knowledge - I and whoever follows me. Glory to Allah, and never will I associate gods with Allah!"' (HQ, 12:108)**

It is obligatory on every believer to unite under these broad-based principles to unite the Islamic world.
These Islamic Missions combine to create **MISSION ISLAM**

'Allah knows best where and how to carry out His Mission.' (HQ, 6:124)

MI1) "WATER IS LIFE" - THE ISLAMIC RELIEF NETWORK - HQ, 21:30

'We made from water every living thing.'
(HQ, 21:30)

MI1) Seeks to increase the access of water and basic health facilities in the Islamic world from 60% to 100%.

THE ISLAMIC WORLD

Health is very important in Islam as the words of Prophet Muhammad (pbuh) show:

'Many people waste two advantages
- health and leisure.'

Poverty and discrimination: the biggest causes of death. The number of children immunities against the six major childhood illnesses grew 5% in 1974 to 80 percent in 1995. However, millions of children still die each year from preventable infectious diseases like diarrhoea, and poor countries still suffer from a lack of heath-care provision.

Muslims must increase their health services and access to safe water. Whilst a few countries do well, the majority are well below average. Most Muslim countries do not have statistics available because the situation is so drastic. Whereas Brunei Darusalaam has 100% of its population with access to water, Afghanistan has only 12%. Whereas Kuwait has 100% of its population with access to health services, Benin only has 18%. Both countries contain Muslims, and both need to be at 100%. Muslims must help each other to establish the Kingdom of Allah.

A basic human right is that you have clean water and access to water, or you cannot survive.

Islamic international relief agencies seek to provide these facilities to the most needy Muslims in a global context, and therefore every Muslim must affiliate themselves with one. They can volunteer their time for helping these people, provide financial help or help these agencies in any way they can.

WATER AND HEALTH ARE THE RIGHTS
OF EVERY MUSLIM

COUNTRIES	% Population - Access to Water	% Population - Access to Health Services
THE KINGDOM OF ALLAH = TARGET	**100**	**100**
THE ISLAMIC WORLD	60	60
AFGHANISTAN	12	29
ALBANIA	Unknown	Unknown
ALGERIA	78	98
AZERBAIJAN	Unknown	Unknown
BAHRAIN	Unknown	98
BANGLADESH	97	45
BENIN	50	18
BOSNIA-HERZGOVINA	Unknown	Unknown
BRUNEI DARUSALAAM	100	100
BURKINA FASO	42	90
CAMEROON	50	80
CHAD	24	30
COMOROS	53	-
DJIBOUTI	90	-
EGYPT	87	99
ERITREA	22	-
ETHIOPIA	25	-
GABON	68	-
GAMBIA	48	93
GUINEA	46	80
GUINEA-BISSAU	59	40
INDONESIA	62	93
IRAN	90	88
IRAQ	78	93
JORDAN	98	97
KAZAKHKSTAN	93	-
KUWAIT	-	100
KYRGYZSTAN	71	-
LEBANON	94	95
LIBYA	97	95
MALAYSIA	78	-
MALDIVES	96	-
MALI	66	40
MAURITANIA	74	63
MOROCCO	65	70
MOZAMBIQUE	63	39
NIGER	48	99
NIGERIA	50	51
OMAN	82	96
PAKISTAN	74	55
QATAR	Unknown	Unknown
SAUDI ARABIA	95	97
SENEGAL	63	90
SIERRA LEONE	34	38
SOMALIA	31	-
SUDAN	50	70
SURINAME	-	-
SYRIA	86	90
TAJIKISTAN	60	-
TANZANIA	38	42
TUNISIA	98	-
TURKEY	49	-
TURKMENISTAN	74	100
UAE	95	99
UGANDA	46	49
UZBEKISTAN	62	-
YEMEN	61	38

MI1) "WATER IS LIFE" - THE ISLAMIC RELIEF NETWORK - HQ, 21:30

THE WEST

The West has all these services in all their areas. The homeless in these countries have a welfare system and can gain basic health and water supplies. The Islamic world must have this as well, and they have been given the wealth to accomplish unity.

COUNTRIES	% Population - Access to Water	% Population - Access to Health Services
AUSTRALIA	100	100
CANADA	100	100
FRANCE	100	100
GERMANY	100	100
ITALY	100	100
UK	100	100
USA	100	100

THE PLAYERS

The Players had many of the same problems that most of the Islamic world had years ago. They did what the Islamic world will do now: PRIORITISED. Once you realise that clean water and health is a priority, you invest in it more and you build it up using your resources.

COUNTRIES	% Population - Access to Water	% Population - Access to Health Services
BRAZIL	93	-
CHINA	67	88
INDIA	81	81
JAPAN	100	100
RUSSIA	Unknown	Unknown

MI1) ISLAMIC MISSION:

Every Muslim must pay their *zakah* (obligatory alms tax) to international Islamic relief agencies, so that the most needy Muslims around the globe get 100% access to water and health facilities.

'Alms are for the poor and the needy, and those employed to administer the funds; and to attract the hearts of those who inclined to Islam; for those in bondage and debt; in the Cause of Allah; and for the wayfarer: a duty ordained by Allah. And Allah is All-Knowing and All-Wise.' (HQ, 9:60)

MI2) "THE BOUNTY OF ALLAH" - THE ISLAMIC COMMERCIAL NETWORK - HQ, 10:58

'In the Bounty of Allah, and in His Mercy - in that, let them rejoice.' (HQ, 10:58)

M12) Seeks the establishment of a global commercial system unifying the Islamic world's resources whereby Muslims trade justly with one another.

THE ISLAMIC WORLD

The Islamic world has the largest and most diverse set of resources in the world. We have every type of industry and good and if we were one united bloc, we would be the richest entity in mankind's history. We have more than 50% of the total world raw materials, 60% of the total mineral resources of the world, including oil, natural gas, gold, silver, copper, zinc, uranium, iron ore, manganese, phosphates etc., and 40% of the world's cotton.

We have 82% of the world's oil reserves, whilst the rest of the world has 18%. We are divided into countries, but must unite now.

POVERTY AND WEALTH

Islam takes a definite stand against poverty, which is declares to be the work of criminals oppressing others. People are responsible for their poverty, though when they suffer from poverty they are worthy of compassion and charity.

Allah commands Muslims to produce wealth, so that we may all live and prosper. We should thank Allah if our efforts succeed, and bear patience if they fail. We hold the decision of Allah and the result achieved on Earth in immense relation. If we succeed, then must do so on our own, for Allah will reward us further.

Every Muslim desires and plans to become a millionaire if we take Islam seriously. We can only amass wealth by earning it in a lawful manner. Islam urges us to produce new wealth and holds the self-made men and entrepreneurs in high esteem.

Islam combats hoarding. If consistently applied to a hoarded wealth, *Zakah* would eat it up in one generation (the years needed for a tax of 2.5% to purchase the stationary capital.)

WHY ARE WE SO POOR?

The Islamic world has all these raw materials, but most of the Muslim countries trade with the West, more than they do with each other. The West takes these raw materials, makes them into manufactured products, and then sells them at a large profit to the Islamic world. That is why the Islamic world has such huge trade deficits, and why the West has none. In some Muslim countries, there are many raw materials which they do not know about, but the West has researched the areas where these are found, and listed them as 'unexploited' - meaning that the West intends to EXPLOIT them. No more exploitation - the Muslims are going to unite and use these resources in a responsible manner to establish the Kingdom of Allah on this Earth.

'It is He sends down rain from the sky, and with it We bring forth all kinds of vegetation.' (HQ, 6:99)

CROPS

Allah's Bounty found in the Islamic world, in our crops - wheat, fruit, vegetables, barley, grapes, olives, grain, cotton, silk, dates, melons, poultry, fisheries, rice, jute, tea, maize, corn, potatoes, bananas, pineapples, sesame seeds, coffee, cocoa, sugar cane, livestock, vanilla, basil, coconuts, market gardening, spices, sugar beet, tomatoes, cucumbers, rubber, palm oil, cloves, cashew nuts, sunflower - the list is huge, all Praise to Allah.

MINERALS

Allah's Bounty found in the Islamic world, in our minerals - iron ore, gas, copper, gold, silver, chromium, uranium, petroleum oil, phosphates, limestone, marble, coal, bauxite manganese, timber, zinc, diamonds, tin ore, granite, platinum, mineral water, mercury, lignite, coral, lithium, gypsum, sulphur, chromate, calcium phosphates, aluminium, mica, lead, sodium sulphate, salt - the list is huge, all Praise to Allah.

INDUSTRIES

Allah's Bounty found in the Islamic world in our industries - carpets, food products, cotton, textiles, food processing, energy generation, machinery, petroleum extraction, chemicals, palm-oil processing, banking, iron, crude steel, electrical appliances, cement, sugar refineries, soap, bicycles, saw-milling, printing, plastics, dairy products, leatherware, glassware, beverages, construction, agricultural processing, wood products, coal, plastic, metal processing, engineering, household appliances, electronics, furniture, clothing, shipping, tourism, motor vehicles, diamonds - the list is huge, all Praise to Allah.

MI2) "THE BOUNTY OF ALLAH" - THE ISLAMIC COMMERCIAL NETWORK - HQ, 10:58

THE WEST

The West's resources in comparison to the Muslim countries shows that it is clear that Muslims are much richer, and as a united bloc, they would be richer than the United States of America and the European Union combined.

After all, what is America if not a centralised system of 51 states, an entire continent, run by the President? The European Union has used the American model and will soon have its own President. The West loves super-states, except the Islamic one.

However, Muslims through sustained effort will try to accomplish this unity through a force which will counter the depravity that is increasing in the world today.

Remember that the West has made some its wealth exploiting the resources of the Islamic world - this exploitation has come to an end.

We will not be held to ransom, nor hold anyone to ransom - we will be righteous, we will be Muslims.

'Verily Allah is full of Bounty to mankind, but most of them are ungrateful.' (HQ, 10:60)

COUNTRIES	CROPS	MINERALS	INDUSTRIES
AUSTRALIA	Wheat, barley, rice, livestock	Coal, iron ore, bauxite, copper, zinc, nickel, uranium, gold, diamonds	Mining, textiles, electrical machinery, mining, media, electronics, tourism, textiles
CANADA	Wheat, barley, livestock	Petroleum, natural gas, coal, copper, nickel, lead, zinc, iron, gold, uranium, timber	Transport equipment, food, paper related products, chemicals
FRANCE	Wheat, sugar beet, maize, vine fruits, livestock	Coal, petroleum, natural gas, iron ore, copper, zinc, bauxite	Mining, quarrying, food products, non- & electrical machinery, weapons, metals, wine, tourism, aircraft
GERMANY	Potatoes, sugar beet, wheat, vine fruits, livestock, fishing	Lignite, hard coal, potash salts, crude oil, natural gas, iron ore, copper, timber, nickel, uranium	Mining, road vehicles, chemicals products, electrical,
ITALY	Sugar beet, grapes, wheat, maize, tomatoes, olives, citrus fruits, vegetables, fishing	Lignite, lead, zinc, mercury, potash, sulphur, bauxite, marble, petroleum, natural gas	Machinery and machine tools. textiles, leather, footwear, food, steel, motor vehicles, chemical products, wine, tourism
UK	Wheat, barley, potatoes, sugar beet, fruit, vegetables, livestock, fishing	Machinery, steel, food processing, aircraft, shipbuilding, petroleum and gas extraction, electronics and communications, business and financial services tourism	Coal, limestone, crude petroleum, natural gas, tin, iron, salt, gravel
USA	Hay, potatoes, maize, wheat, barley, soya beans, citrus, fruit, cotton, livestock	Coal, copper, iron, bauxite, mercury, silver, gold, nickel, zinc, tungsten, uranium, phosphate, petroleum, natural gas, timber	Machinery, petroleum refining and products, food processing, motor vehicles, pig iron, steel, chemical products, electrical goods, printing and publishing

THE PLAYERS

Many of the Players have developing economies which will play a strong part in the future, and these must be aware of the competition the USA and the European Union places on them.

COUNTRIES	CROPS	MINERALS	INDUSTRIES
BRAZIL	Coffee, soya beans, tobacco, sugar cane, cocoa beans, livestock	Iron ore, tin, aluminium, gold, phosphates, platinum, uranium	Mining, steel, machinery, textiles, clothing, petrochemicals
CHINA	Sweet potatoes, wheat, marble, rice, cotton, fish	Coal, graphite, tungsten, tin, lead, iron ore, diamonds, gold, manganese, zinc	Cotton, cement, paper., sugar, plastics, aluminium ware, steel, silk, woollen fabrics, cameras, electrical appliances, tourism
INDIA	Cotton, tea, wheat, rice, coffee, cashew nuts, jute, spices, sugar cane, oil seeds	Coal, iron ore, copper ore, bauxite, chromite, gold, manganese, crude oil, natural gas, diamonds	Mining, manufacturing, shipbuilding, road transport, cotton cloth, sugar
JAPAN	Rice, potatoes, cabbages, citrus fruit, fish	Coal, zinc, iron, copper, natural, gas	Motor vehicles, steel machinery, electrical and electronic equipment, chemicals, textiles
RUSSIA	Grain, potatoes, flax, vegetables	Petroleum, natural gas, coal, peat, copper, iron ore, lead, aluminium, phosphate rock, nickel, manganese, gold, diamonds	Cast iron, steel, rolled iron, synthetic fibres, soap, cellulose, paper, paper, cement, glass, bricks, food-processing, confectionery

MI2) ISLAMIC MISSION:

Everyone involved in business, be they a barber or an international corporation must agree to conduct all business with each other justly according to Islamic ethics and to try to implement all Islamic Missions.

'Then did we granted you victory over them. And we increased your resources and sons, and made you more numerous in man-power.' (HQ, 17:6)

MI3) "WAR ON USURY" - THE ISLAMIC FINANCIAL NETWORK - HQ, 2:278-9

M13) Seeks to eliminate the Islamic world's debt through the establishment of a global financial and banking system based on Islamic law.

'O you who believe! Fear Allah and eliminate usury if you are really believers. And if you do not, then take notice of a war from Allah and His Messenger.' (HQ, 2:278-9)

THE ISLAMIC WORLD

It is known as the infinite debt spiral. Internal negotiations to reduce and eliminate Third World debt have only led to increasing exports of capital and further debt of the countries affected (as with sub-Saharan Africa). The wealthy North has established a new form of economic colonialism, a new version of the old "debt bondage". The Islamic world are slaves to the evil banking system.

Criminals have profited from this evil banking system by charging extortionate interest on loans to countries who want to develop their countries, though Allah has forbidden usury.

Any loans which the political leadership of the Islamic world are the obligation of the Muslims to pay, even when this leadership is changed.

An International Islamic Banking system is being set up where all Muslims will be able to bank according to Islamic law, where usury is forbidden. However, trained personnel is lacking. Muslims must be good Muslims and study Islam proficiently, and learn about the present banking system, and provide the Islamic alternative.

Islamic banks are being established and are growing stronger in the international banking system. There has to be strong evidence that the activities of Islamic Banking are monitored by those who have studied Islam in detail, and can provide sincere advice on what is lawful and unlawful for Muslims to invest in. It is a fact that non-Muslims are now investing in Islamic Banking, perceiving it to be an excellent long-term investment, which shows that Islam is the best system in this world, for the overall betterment of humanity.

This will mean that the Islamic world will no longer be in this infinite debt spiral, and neither will the rest of the Earth.

COUNTRIES	TOTAL EXTERNAL DEBT IN MILLIONS $
THE KINGDOM OF ALLAH = TARGET	0
THE ISLAMIC WORLD	70549.2
AFGHANISTAN	9580
ALBANIA	781
ALGERIA	33260
AZERBAIJAN	435
BAHRAIN	2960
BANGLADESH	16083
BENIN	1594
BOSNIA- HERZGOVINA	3400
BRUNEI DARUSALAAM	-
BURKINA FASO	1294
CAMEROON	9515
CHAD	997
COMOROS	190
DJIBOUTI	247
EGYPT	31407
ERITREA	46
ETHIOPIA	10077
GABON	4213
GAMBIA	452
GUINEA	3240
GUINEA-BISSAU	937
INDONESIA	129033
IRAN	21183
IRAQ	100400
JORDAN	8118
KAZAKHKSTAN	2920
KUWAIT	5800
KYRGYZSTAN	789
LEBANON	3996
LIBYA	4200
MALAYSIA	39777
MALDIVES	162
MALI	3020
MAURITANIA	2363
MOROCCO	21767
MOZAMBIQUE	5842
NIGER	1557
NIGERIA	31407
OMAN	3415
PAKISTAN	29901
QATAR	6350
SAUDI ARABIA	17800
SENEGAL	3663
SIERRA LEONE	1167
SOMALIA	2610
SUDAN	16972
SURINAME	68.2
SYRIA	21420
TAJIKISTAN	707
TANZANIA	7412
TUNISIA	9887
TURKEY	79789
TURKMENISTAN	825
UAE	17
UGANDA	3674
UZBEKISTAN	2319
YEMEN	6356

MI3) "WAR ON USURY" - <u>THE ISLAMIC FINANCIAL NETWORK</u> - HQ, 2:278-9

THE WEST

If all of the West was to conduct business and financing without usury, there would be more prosperity and it would be lawful as well. So they may not have external debts, but the citizens of these countries do not want to be part of a system which exploits the rest of the world, and so interest rates as part of economic policy must be eliminated.

The West have their wealth in their countries divided in an unjust way. If justice is the prime basis for economic activity, then there will be lower taxes, increases in wages, greater social justice and happiness.

'So whoever receives admonition from his Lord and stops eating usury shall not be punished for the past; but whoever returns to usury, such are the dwellers of the Fire - they will abide there forever.'
(HQ, 2:275)

COUNTRIES	TOTAL EXTERNAL DEBT IN MILLIONS $
AUSTRALIA	Unlisted
CANADA	Unlisted
FRANCE	Unlisted
GERMANY	Unlisted
ITALY	Unlisted
UK	Unlisted
USA	Unlisted

THE PLAYERS

It is the duty of all these countries, who have been the victims of the international banking system to look at the only viable and sound alternative - Islamic Finance. This will fairness and justice will be present all over the globe.

COUNTRIES	TOTAL EXTERNAL DEBT IN MILLIONS $
BRAZIL	179047
CHINA	128817
INDIA	89827
JAPAN	Unlisted
RUSSIA	124785

MI3) ISLAMIC MISSION

Muslims must strive to provide an International Islamic Banking system. Businesses must agree to do business without usury, and so must individuals. This means change - changing everything from bank accounts to investments, must all be done to Islamic law. The alternative system is coming and it will bring justice around the globe.

'Allah will destroy usury and will compensate for charity in His Name. And Allah does not like disbelievers and sinners.' (HQ, 2:276)

MI4) "READ!" - THE ISLAMIC LITERACY NETWORK - HQ, 96:1

'Read! In the Name of your Lord Who has created.'
(HQ, 96:1)

MI4) Seeks to increase the Islamic world's literacy rate from 61% to 100%.

THE ISLAMIC WORLD

It is ironic that the first world that the Prophet Muhammad (pbuh) received from Allah was 'Read' - not once, but three times. Therefore, it is sad that today over half a billion Muslims are illiterate.

Education is a basic human right, for men and women. It is sad to see that in some Muslim countries, the number of men who can read is double that of women - women have as much right to read as men, and this is the Law of Allah. Some Muslim countries are much more literate than others, so it not as if this is an impossible mission. If Azerbaijan can have 100% literacy, then so can Burkina Faso, Eritrea and Niger.

There are huge variations in the number of teachers in schools compared to the pupils. This is because teaching is considered today in the Islamic world as a profession that does not pay well and does not command respect. Teaching is considered to be a sign of nobility and honour in Islam. It should be encouraged as a profession around the world.

Therefore, it is imperative that the targets for the Islamic world are reached. Every single person in the Islamic world must know how to read and write. The number of teachers in schools should be increased and more women should become literate so they can teach their children. Everyone Muslim must be able to read the Holy Qur'an in Arabic and in their native languages.

The Prophet (pbuh) said:
'You should acquire all the wisdom of which you are capable! But Allah will not reward you for all that until you translate it into actions!'

COUNTRIES	% Literate Total	% Adult Males Literate	% Adult Females Literate	Primary pupil : Teacher
THE KINGDOM OF ALLAH = TARGET	**100**	**100**	**100**	**5-9**
THE ISLAMIC WORLD	**61**	**79**	**52**	**50**
AFGHANISTAN	32	47	15	-
ALBANIA	-	-	-	18
ALGERIA	62	74	49	27
AZERBAIJAN	100	100	99	20
BAHRAIN	85	89	79	-
BANGLADESH	38	49	26	-
BENIN	37	49	26	49
BOSNIA-HERZGOVINA	90	90	90	-
BRUNEI DARUSALAAM	88	93	83	-
BURKINA FASO	19	30	9	58
CAMEROON	63	75	52	46
CHAD	48	62	35	62
COMOROS	57	64	50	-
DJIBOUTI	46	60	33	-
EGYPT	51	64	39	24
ERITREA	15	22.5	7.5	41
ETHIOPIA	36	50	20	33
GABON	63	74	53	52
GAMBIA	39	53	25	30
GUINEA	36	50	22	49
GUINEA-BISSAU	55	68	43	-
INDONESIA	84	90	78	23
IRAN	69	78	59	32
IRAQ	58	71	45	22
JORDAN	87	93	79	21
KAZAKHKSTAN	100	100	98	20
KUWAIT	79	82	75	15
KYRGYZSTAN	97	99	95	20
LEBANON	92	95	90	12
LIBYA	76	88	63	-
MALAYSIA	84	89	78	20
MALDIVES	93	93	93	-
MALI	31	39	23	66
MAURITANIA	38	50	26	52
MOROCCO	44	57	31	28
MOZAMBIQUE	40	58	23	-
NIGER	14	21	7	37
NIGERIA	57	67	47	37
OMAN	59	71	46	26
PAKISTAN	38	50	24	-
QATAR	79	79	80	-
SAUDI ARABIA	63	72	50	13
SENEGAL	33	43	23	-
SIERRA LEONE	31	45	18	-
SOMALIA	24	36	14	-
SUDAN	46	58	35	36
SURINAME	93	95	91	-
SYRIA	71	86	56	24
TAJIKISTAN	100	100	100	23
TANZANIA	68	79	57	37
TUNISIA	67	79	55	25
TURKEY	82	92	72	28
TURKMENISTAN	98	99	97	-
UAE	79	79	80	-
UGANDA	62	74	50	35
UZBEKISTAN	100	100	100	21
YEMEN	33	53	26	-

MI4) "READ!" - THE ISLAMIC LITERACY NETWORK - HQ, 96:1

THE WEST

It is ironic that the culture which does not obey Allah has really understood the statement : READ! Everyone in these countries can read and write, and they all have many teachers for those wishing to learn. It is strange that those who do not believe in Allah have used His concept to acquire knowledge to make them the dominant culture. Muslims must realise that the West is mimicking the success of the Islamic world by acquiring knowledge. But knowledge is nothing, unless one realises that Allah is He whom all this knowledge emanates from.

COUNTRIES	% Literate Total	% Adult Males Literate	% Adult Females Literate	Primary pupil: Teacher Ratio
AUSTRALIA	99	99	99	16
CANADA	99	99	99	16
FRANCE	100	100	100	19
GERMANY	100	100	100	18
ITALY	98	99	98	11
JAPAN	99	99	99	18
UK	99	99	99	19
USA	99	99	99	16

The worlds top producers of books are the UK, China. Germany and America. Thus, we will only know when the Muslims are stronger if they are dominating this list. So publish in all media, from books to the Internet, so just knowledge and ideas can spread.

This is the key - the moment you have great knowledge, you have great power, which means great responsibility to strive for justice: **'Knowledge is Power - Power is Responsibility for Justice.'**

However, in the West, education is in crisis. Transformed by scientific and technological revolutions into a means of adapting individuals to the globalised market, it has strayed form its original principles of forming citizens fully capable of participating in communities. This is a warning Muslims should heed - become citizens in communities who strive for justice.

THE PLAYERS

Make literacy and education a priority - whilst heeding the harmful effects that science and technology have had on the West's form of education. From knowledge, comes justice and justice is Allah's Command.

COUNTRIES	% Literate Total	% Adult Males Literate	% Adult Females Literate	Primar y pupil : Teacher Ratio
BRAZIL	68	79	57	37
CHINA	82	90	73	24
INDIA	52	66	38	63
JAPAN	99	99	99	18
RUSSIA	99	100	99	20

MI4) ISLAMIC MISSION:

All Muslims must increase the literacy rate in the Islamic world from 61% to 100% by offering time, skills and wealth to achieve this. Depending on each Muslim's own capacity, they can send money to Islamic educational funds, send old textbooks to schools in the Islamic world, learning programmes - help to make the Muslims literate through just means.

MI5) "SIGNS IN LANGUAGES" - <u>THE ISLAMIC LINGUISTIC NETWORK</u> - HQ, 30:22

'And among His signs are the creation of the heavens and the Earth and the differences of your languages and colours. Verily, in that are indeed signs for men of sound knowledge.' (HQ, 30:22)

M15) Seeks to have the Invitation to Islam in every language and for the world to understand the Holy Qur'an in their native language and in Arabic.

THE ISLAMIC WORLD

Look at the variety of languages that the Islamic world: Arabic, Hausa, Berber, Urdu, Albanian, Chinese, Russian to English, Spanish and French.

Arabic is considered the language of Islam because it is the language of the Holy Qur'an. However, throughout the day we speak in our own languages. Those whose ancestry is Arab now speak perhaps in Spanish because they live in Spain or in Sicily they speak in Italian. But, our unity is shown that when we worship Allah, the Almighty, everyone around the world prays in Arabic. They all believe that 'There is no God but Allah and that Muhammad is His Messenger.'

The Holy Qur'an is printed in all these languages but all Invitation to Islam must all be printed in this style. Talk to these people in the language and style that they will love Islam and Allah best in. Speak and write in Albanian to an Albanian and French and Wolof to the Senegalese and invite them to Islam. Talk in a style that they will like Islam in - place the concept of Allah, being the Most Merciful and Compassionate first and helping them to understand that they should follow His Way.

All Muslims must increase their knowledge of Arabic. The moment they do that their lives change for the better. They will understand the beauty of the Holy Qur'an so much more, and their worship to Allah will become much more beautiful than it already is. To know Allah better, the Holy Qur'an is primary, and as it is in Arabic, learn Arabic. To Allah, is the Final Destination.

The Prophet (pbuh)

'Make matters easy rather than difficult. Show people the bright side of things rather than the hateful ones. Preach in a moderate and direct way.'

COUNTRIES	LANGUAGES
THE KINGDOM OF ALLAH = TARGET	**MAIN - QUR'ANIC ARABIC ISLAMIC ENGLISH**
THE ISLAMIC WORLD	**MANY**
AFGHANISTAN	Pushtu, Dari, Persian, Uzbek, Kirgiz
ALBANIA	Albanian
ALGERIA	Arabic, French, Berber
AZERBAIJAN	Azerbaijani
BAHRAIN	Arabic, English, Urdu, Farsi
BANGLADESH	Bengali, English
BENIN	French, Fon, Yoruba
BOSNIA- HERZGOVINA	Bosnian
BRUNEI DARUSALAAM	Malay, Chinese (Hokkien), English
BURKINA FASO	French, 50 Sudanic languages
CAMEROON	French, Arabic, Sudanic languages
CHAD	French, Arabic
COMOROS	Arabic, Comorian, Makua, French
DJIBOUTI	French, Somali, Afar, Arabic
EGYPT	Arabic, English, French
ERITREA	Amharic, Tigrinya, Arabic
ETHIOPIA	Amharic, Tigrinya, Arabic
GABON	French, Fang, Myene
GAMBIA	English, Mandinka, Fula
GUINEA	French, 8 African Languages
GUINEA-BISSAU	Portuguese, Spanish, English
INDONESIA	Bahama Indonesia, Javanese
IRAN	Farsi, Kurdish, Turkish, Arabic
IRAQ	Arabic, Kurdish
JORDAN	Arabic, English
KAZAKHKSTAN	Kazakh, Russian
KUWAIT	Arabic, Kurdish, Farsi, English
KYRGYZSTAN	Kyrgyz
LEBANON	Arabic, French, English
LIBYA	Arabic
MALAYSIA	Malay, English, Chinese
MALDIVES	Dhivehi
MALI	French , Bambara
MAURITANIA	Arabic, Berber, French
MOROCCO	Arabic, French
MOZAMBIQUE	Portuguese, 16 African languages
NIGER	French, Hausa, Djerma
NIGERIA	English, Hausa, Ibo, Yoruba
OMAN	Arabic, English, Urdu
PAKISTAN	Urdu, English, local dialects
QATAR	Arabic, English
SAUDI ARABIA	Arabic, English
SENEGAL	French, Wolof
SIERRA LEONE	English, Krio
SOMALIA	Arabic, Somali, Italian, English
SUDAN	Arabic and others
SURINAME	Spanish, Durch, English, Hindi, Javanese, Chinese
SYRIA	Arabic, Kurdish, Armenian
TAJIKISTAN	Tajik
TANZANIA	Kiswahili, English
TUNISIA	Arabic, French
TURKEY	Turkish, Kurdish, Arabic
TURKMENISTAN	Turkman, Russian
UAE	Arabic, Farsi, Hindi, Urdu, English
UGANDA	English, Kiswahili, Bantu and Niolitic
UZBEKISTAN	Uzbek
YEMEN	Arabic

MI5) "SIGNS IN LANGUAGES" - THE ISLAMIC LINGUISTIC NETWORK - HQ, 30:22

THE WEST

English is the language of power - international business, commerce and diplomacy. It is the highest spoken language in the world with 1,200 million speakers - after that it is Mandarin, Hindi/Urdu, Spanish, Russian, Arabic, Bengali, Portuguese, Malay/Indonesian, Japanese, German and French.

However, English is the dominant language, with the English of England considered the best. All Muslims know some English at the very least, mainly due to being part of the Commonwealth, television and now the Internet. All the latest technology such as on the Internet is in English. Therefore, it is important that after their own native language and Qur'anic Arabic, English must be learned to a level.

The future of Islam means that English as a language is changing and evolving as it always has done, but its tone and style and words are showing the impact of Islam. Common day language and international business are being conducted in this Islamic English whereby words such as Allah, Salaam, Zakah, Riba and Inshallah are being incorporated into the language. The English we use today is becoming Islamic English.

COUNTRIES	LANGUAGES
AUSTRALIA	English
CANADA	English, French
FRANCE	French
GERMANY	German
ITALY	Italian, German, French
UK	English
USA	English, Spanish

THE PLAYERS

Muslims must try to learn the languages of these countries, so that Islam can spread around the globe.

COUNTRIES	LANGUAGES
BRAZIL	Portugeuse, Spanish, English
CHINA	Chinese - Mandarin, Cantonese, Wu
INDIA	Hindi, Urdu, English and 16 other languages
JAPAN	Japanese, Ainu
RUSSIA	Russian

MI5) ISLAMIC MISSION

It is the duty of every Muslim to understand the Holy Qur'an in Arabic, and also in their native language. It is the duty of Muslims who perform Invitation to Islam missions to learn the languages of the world, and make Islam global. English, the language of worldly power, through the language of Muslims around the world must become Islamic English, whereby the Power of Allah is seen.

'We sent not a Messenger except in the language of his own people, in order to make things clear to them.' (HQ, 14:4)

MI6) "GENERATION ISLAM" - THE ISLAMIC GENERATIONS NETWORK - HQ, 11:116

MI6) Seeks to increase the youth in the Islamic world's commitment to Islam through Mission Islam across the generations.

'If only they had been of the generations before you who had wisdom, who prohibited men from mischief in the Earth.' (HQ, 11:116)

THE ISLAMIC WORLD

'We heard a youth talk of them: he is called Abraham.' (HQ, 21:60)

Muslims have increased by a staggering amount because of their population, and this has meant that the number of youths in every Muslim country is nearly 50%. For every child, there is 1 adult, but in the West, for every child, there is 6 adults. This in the future means that the West will be old and the Muslim countries new, strong, young and dynamic.

Young populations in the Islamic world will have energy, vibrancy, dynamism, and encourage political assertiveness. History has taught us this - when the young, naive and idealistic learn of Islam, and look at the world around them, they will want to change it. Islamic change is the same as dynamism and vibrancy - this is Generation Islam.

However, the future also means that in the Islamic world, as compared to 1990, in the year 2010, entrants to the job markets will increase by about 50%. The unemployment problem, so awful that Muslim countries do not publish this statistic, will become even more intolerable - unless the Muslim countries employ the laws of Islam and unite.

The youth must therefore interact with the elders and scholars of Islam who educate them about Islam, with their wisdom and experience. They must show them that it is important to learn from the mistakes of the past, and to try to improve our future position based upon Allah's Laws.

The wisdom and experience of our elders will combine with the dynamism and vibrancy of the youth in the Islamic world to make them strong. But they must remember that inner strength must match outer strength for as the Prophet (pbuh) said:

'The strong man is not the one who throw people in wrestling. The strong man is the one who has control over himself when he is angry.'

COUNTRIES	% POPULATION UNDER 15 YEARS OF AGE
THE KINGDOM OF ALLAH = TARGET	**GENERATION ISLAM**
THE ISLAMIC WORLD	**DYNAMIC AND IDEALISTIC**
AFGHANISTAN	40
ALBANIA	31
ALGERIA	38
AZERBAIJAN	31
BAHRAIN	32
BANGLADESH	39
BENIN	47
BOSNIA-HERZGOVINA	22
BRUNEI DARUSALAAM	34
BURKINA FASO	44
CAMEROON	44
CHAD	43
COMOROS	49
DJIBOUTI	42
EGYPT	38
ERITREA	-
ETHIOPIA	-
GABON	39
GAMBIA	41
GUINEA	47
GUINEA-BISSAU	41
INDONESIA	33
IRAN	43
IRAQ	43
JORDAN	43
KAZAKHKSTAN	29
KUWAIT	39
KYRGYZSTAN	37
LEBANON	34
LIBYA	45
MALAYSIA	38
MALDIVES	47
MALI	47
MAURITANIA	43
MOROCCO	36
MOZAMBIQUE	37
NIGER	48
NIGERIA	46
OMAN	47
PAKISTAN	44
QATAR	40
SAUDI ARABIA	41
SENEGAL	44
SIERRA LEONE	44
SOMALIA	47
SUDAN	43
SURINAME	35
SYRIA	47
TAJIKISTAN	43
TANZANIA	34
TUNISIA	34
TURKEY	33
TURKMENISTAN	39
UAE	31
UGANDA	48
UZBEKISTAN	39
YEMEN	46

MI6) "GENERATION ISLAM" - THE ISLAMIC GENERATIONS NETWORK - HQ, 11:116

THE WEST

America and Europe have increasingly aging populations. Medical advances ensure an average lifetime in the high seventies.

However, these elderly people do not have longer ACTIVE lifetimes. At the turn of the 20th century, a Westerner could expect to spend an average of the last 2 years of life as an invalid. Today, the figure is 7 years.

But though medicine prolongs life, it does not prolong mobility nearly as well. Therefore, these people may be alive but the quality of their lives goes down for that period, and many are in old people's homes. This means that they become a socio-economic burden as well.

We must take care of our elderly, for they are the ones who have wisdom and the greatest experience to impart. We must not allow them to suffer immobile with a low quality of life. They must be cared for by the family in their old age.

The West should treasure the aged and young in proportion not one over the other - only Islam will show them how they can do this.

COUNTRIES	% POPULATION UNDER 15 YEARS OF AGE
AUSTRALIA	21
CANADA	20
FRANCE	19
GERMANY	16
ITALY	15
UK	19
USA	22

THE PLAYERS

These countries should treasure the aged and young in proportion, and to ensure that their future generation is successful, they must be exposed to the benefits of Islam.

COUNTRIES	% POPULATION UNDER 15 YEARS OF AGE
BRAZIL	32
CHINA	26
INDIA	35
JAPAN	16
RUSSIA	21

MI6) ISLAMIC MISSION:

The Islamic World with its youthful population explosion will mean that idealist youth with the help older, wiser more experienced Muslim elders, must acquire knowledge about spreading Islam and use their energy as Generation Islam to establish Allah's Kingdom.

'We gave him wisdom even as a youth.'
(HQ, 19:12)

MI7) "PLANET ISLAM" - THE ISLAMIC GLOBAL NETWORK - HQ, 12:108

**'Say: "This is My Way:
I invite unto Allah with sound knowledge –
I and whoever follows me.
Glory to Allah,
and never will I associate gods with Allah!"'
(HQ, 12:108)**

M17) Seeks to promote True Islam to 4.5 billion people on this Earth in the most suitable manner.

THE ISLAMIC WORLD

The forecast of Samuel Huntingdon in 'The Clash of Civilisations'

'The percentage of Christians in the world peaked at about 30 percent in the 1980s, levelled off, is now declining, and will probably approximate about 25% of the world's population by 2025. As a result of their extremely high rates of population growth, the proportion of Muslims in the world will continue to increase dramatically, amounting to 20 percent of the world's population about the turn of the century, surpassing the number of Christians some years later, and probably accounting for about 30 percent of the world's population by 2025.'

There are a 1,500,000,000 Muslims in the world today, and they are living side by side with non-Muslim minorities and treating them well.

Every country has a Muslim presence - notable populations include Argentina, Belgium, Bhutan, Chechnya, Dagestan (Muslim countries, part of Islamic World), Denmark, Finland, Bulgaria, Burundi, Cambodia, Central African Republic, Congo, Fiji, Ghana, Greece, Guyana, Kenya, Liberia, Madagascar, Malawi, Mauritius, Myanmar, Nepal, Netherlands, New Caledonia, Norway, Phillipines, Poland, Portugal, Rwanda, Singapore, South Africa, Spain, Sri Lanka, Sweden, Switzerland, Thailand, Trinidad & Tobago, Zaire and Zambia. It is possible that these minorities could become majorities very quickly.

It is the duty of every Muslim to act as an ambassador for Allah. Whomever they meet and wherever, be it the gardener or the business executive, needs to know the reason for there existence and are potential Muslims. Invitation to Islam through personal example is best, and Muslims need to be proud of their religion as they once were - we have the Truth.

COUNTRIES	% POPULATIONS MUSLIM
THE KINGDOM OF ALLAH = TARGET	**100%**
THE ISLAMIC WORLD	**25% WORLD POPULATION**
AFGHANISTAN	100
ALBANIA	70
ALGERIA	100
AZERBAIJAN	88
BAHRAIN	85
BANGLADESH	85
BENIN	15
BOSNIA- HERZGOVINA	55
BRUNEI DARUSALAAM	66
BURKINA FASO	36
CAMEROON	33
CHAD	45
COMOROS	100
DJIBOUTI	100
EGYPT	96
ERITREA	45
ETHIOPIA	50
GABON	1
GAMBIA	90
GUINEA	95
GUINEA-BISSAU	38
INDONESIA	90
IRAN	97
IRAQ	98
JORDAN	92
KAZAKHKSTAN	100
KUWAIT	99
KYRGYZSTAN	100
LEBANON	58
LIBYA	100
MALAYSIA	85
MALDIVES	100
MALI	90
MAURITANIA	85
MOROCCO	99
MOZAMBIQUE	16
NIGER	70
NIGERIA	70
OMAN	99
PAKISTAN	96
QATAR	44
SAUDI ARABIA	100
SENEGAL	95
SIERRA LEONE	39
SOMALIA	100
SUDAN	75
SURINAME	20
SYRIA	92
TAJIKISTAN	40
TANZANIA	100
TUNISIA	96
TURKEY	100
TURKMENISTAN	100
UAE	96
UGANDA	100
UZBEKISTAN	100
YEMEN	100

MI7) "PLANET ISLAM" - THE ISLAMIC GLOBAL NETWORK - HQ, 12:108

THE WEST

There is much work to be done in the West by Muslims for Muslims and the non-Muslims. Invitation to Islam must be conducted effectively as has been outlined. Agnostics, atheists and humanists are increasing in the West and around the globe. Therefore, Invitation to Islam must be done by the Muslims in the West to reduce and eventually eliminate this lack of belief.

COUNTRIES	% POPULATION MUSLIMS
AUSTRALIA	2
CANADA	1
FRANCE	6
GERMANY	3
ITALY	2
UK	4
USA	5

In the UK, 'The Times' gave this reason why British women are becoming Muslims:
'Westerners despairing of their own society - rising in crime, family breakdown, drugs and alcoholism - have come to admire the discipline and security of Islam. Many converts are former Christians disillusioned by the uncertainty of the church and unhappy with the concept of the Trinity and the deification of Jesus.'

THE PLAYERS

Invitation to Islam is global, and is important to these nations. Every Muslim, be they a businessman there or Muslims born in those countries, must work to make these countries part of the Islamic world.

COUNTRIES	% POPULATION MUSLIMS
BRAZIL	1
CHINA	11
INDIA	18
JAPAN	1
RUSSIA	2

'We can all, as never before,
peer into each other's worlds.
Such a capacity makes it crucial
hat we have the understanding to see through
the veil of prejudice and cultural differences
to grasp the common thread of humanity we all share.'

MI7) ISLAMIC MISSION

Muslims must begin to see every non-Muslim they meet as a potential Muslim - be it a clerk or the President. Invite to Islam in the way prescribed by the Prophet (pbuh) and be proud of being Muslims. 4.5 billion people who were born Muslims can go into the Hereafter as Muslims inshallah, but we need to deliver the Message to each and everyone one of them.

'O mankind! We have created you from a male and a female, and made you into nations and tribes, that you may know one another. Verily, the most honourable of you with Allah is those who have piety and love good deeds. Indeed, Allah is All-Knowing, All-Aware.'
(HQ, 49:13)

THE FUTURE : THE PLANNED & THE PROPHESIED

Some of these issues are reality, some have been prophesied by the Prophet (pbuh) and others are on the agenda - they may materialise, they may not - the fact they are possible, being planned for and increasingly imminent, makes them important.

Politics	- The Corrupt, Tyrannical, Debauched and Disbelieving Rule - The Coming of the False Messiah, the Anti-Christ
Economics	- Increase divide between the Rich and Poor - Debts increase
Social	- Depression, Paranoia, Confusion, Loneliness - Sexual Immorality on an unprecedented scale
Justice	- The Wrong is enjoined - evil is given a legal right - 'Justice' is Blind to The Truth.
Education	- Knowledge is sought for wealth and power, for immoral means by immoral means
Culture	- The unlawful influences the lawful, the changes are devastating.
Science & Technology	- Genetic engineering, legalisation of eugenics, the race of robots, human cloning, hybrids, colonisation of Mars and the Moon, nanotechnology, international space stations, space cities, mutant germs and bacteria - used by criminals for evil.
Environment	- Natural and Technological Disasters means the Earth is scarred beyond repair.
Defense	- Increased World Conflict with Humanity the sufferer
Models	- The Disbeliever is the Role Model of the Innocent Child
Religion	- Personalised Religion - MAN BELIEVES HE IS GOD

All plans are subject to Allah's Will - that is what all must realise. These plans all have a component in which they realise their greatest potential or if their basis is evil, never begin - that is the Islamic component.

Unity can be achieved on the broad-based principles of Mission Islam -
there is no compulsion in Islam.

THE ANSWER TO ALL THESE ISSUES OF THE FUTURE

MILLENNIUM ISLAM

If the New World Order heralds the advent of the False Messiah

Then the Kingdom of Allah heralds the advent of the Real Messiah

YOUR GUIDED LEADER

Now the time has come. Praise be to Allah - the solution to the world's current and future problems.

Let us start with the Muslims. Now what is missing here is Leadership. Since the time of the Prophet (pbuh) in AD 632, Muslims have had a leader called a Caliph who was the head of the Islamic Ummah and his role was to defend and propagate the faith of Islam all over the globe. Officially, the Caliphate was abolished on 3rd March 1924 - in the same day in 1999, heralded its 75th anniversary. Indeed, a time to think, reflect and ACT.

> The Messenger of Allah (pbuh) said 'The **Prophethood** will remain among you for as long as Allah wills, then Allah will remove it when He wishes to remove it. Then there will be a **Caliphate on the method of the Prophethood,** it will last as long as Allah wishes. Then Allah will remove it when He wishes. Then it will be a **hereditary leadership** which will last as long as Allah wills. Then Allah will remove it when He wishes. Then there will be **tyrannical rule**, and it will remain so for as long as Allah wills. Then Allah will remove it when He wishes. Then there will be a **Caliphate on the method of the Prophethood**. ' Then, he kept silent.

> Anyone who has read that will infer that the Caliphate finished after the end of the Caliphs who Took the Right Path, Ali bin Abu Talib (656-661 AD).

> After him was Mu'awiya (661-680 AD) who gave the leadership to his son, Yazid (680-683 AD) making it hereditary.

> Soon after that you have tyrannical rule over Muslims in one form or another up until the present day. Therefore, we are currently preparing for the return of the Caliphate.

Le Gai Eaton's analysis of the leader of Islam raises the most important points:

> The Muslims have taken a very pragmatic view of the ruler's function. He is not expected to be a saint or sage or even a good man in the usual sense of the term, and his private vices may be overlooked so long as they are kept private.

> What is required of him is that **he should have a strong right arm with which to defend the community against its enemies and to maintain the Law.** It is often said that **Muslims prefer a strong and even ruthless man** to a gentle and conciliatory one. If this is so, it is because **a ruthless man is likely to be more effective in fulfilling the function allotted to him in the Islamic system.** Most human communities throughout history have lived precariously, surrounded by enemies on every side and they cannot give proper attention to the worship of God, or get on with the business of living, unless **they are able to rely upon an effective protector.**

> Pious Muslims have always regarded **power as a fearful thing**, even as a **one-way ticket to hell**; profiting from the protection afforded them by the ruler and from the good order he established in the city, **they thank God that someone else bears this burden and walks this tightrope over the abyss. They suspect that there must be a profound flaw in the character of anyone who deliberately seeks to expose to himself to the dangers and temptation of power.**

The Prophet (pbuh) said
'Do not ask for leadership for if you are given much power as a result of asking for it you will be left to deal with it on your own; **but if you are given it without your asking, then you will be helped in exercising it.'**

**'If power is thrust upon a man, he may be forgiven much;
but if he chooses to put a noose around his own neck, he is likely to hang by it.'**

All around us -
the rulers, whether they are democratic politicians or military dictators,
hold power because they deliberately sought power and believed themselves fit to wield it.

THE PROPHET MUHAMMAD (PBUH) : THE MODEL LEADER

These are the attributes we know which make a good leader, on a village/town/province/state/national/global level.

THE REALISTIC MAN

Your leader should be realistic - his messages and demands should not be in contradiction with the realities of life. He should consider the conditions surrounding your community as it actually is.

HE WHO SELF-EVALUATES

He should be aware of the advantages and disadvantages he has.

THE CONVINCED OPTIMIST

Your leader should be convinced of the truth of the message he conveys to you all. He should never falter in his convictions and be firm in conveying his message without giving up. A leader who frequently changes opinions causes rifts and disagreements among his community.

THE BRAVE

Your leader should be courageous in nature. Even left alone to himself, he should find as much courage as to resists all the difficulties he may encounter.

STRONG WILL-POWER

Your leader should have strong will-power and resolve and never fall into hopelessness.

A RESPONSIBLE MAN

Your leader should be aware of his responsibility and nothing should be able to prevent him from fulfilling it. Especially the charms of the world and the attractions of life should not be able to intervene between him and his responsibility.

A MAN WITH VISION

Your leader should be forward-looking and thinking and have determined his goal well. He should have the mental capacity to discern the developments he may encounter in the future. He should also be able to evaluate the past, the present and the future together and reach new syntheses.

KNOWS THE RIGHTEOUS

Your leader should be able to identify the righteous and skilled men to aid him in his responsibilities. He should be a good and accurate judge of character and should know his close team's dispositions, character, abilities, shortcomings, ambitions and flaws individually. This will enable him especially to make the best choice in his appointments to important offices. At a community level, he should know the members of the community individually. On a global scale, he should know the righteous members of the global community individually.

STRONG CHARACTER AND ADMIRABLE

Your leader should have a strong character and be equipped with praiseworthy virtues. He should be determined in carrying out his decisions but capable of flexibility; he should know when to be firm and forceful; when to be relenting and compassionate. He should be serious and dignified, but modest. He should be upright, truthful, trustworthy, knowledgeable and just.

A MAN FROM AMONGST YOU

He should not abuse his power. He should live like an ordinary man and never discriminate among his citizens. He should love all of them, prefer them over himself and be able to make himself loved by them sincerely. He should be faithful to you all and be able to secure your loyalty and devotion.

Do your leaders measure up to this? They will - if you make those men with these qualities your leaders. Force your allegiance on those whom you believe have these qualities.

In the Millennium, Muslims need a leader and this how you will know him:

CRITERIA FOR THE LEADER OF MUSLIMS IN THE MILLENNIUM

He is a pious and brave Muslim

His duty to Allah and his responsibilities are above ANYTHING

He defends and propagates Islam

He establishes the Sovereignty of Allah on this Earth

He is accountable to Allah and every Muslim he governs.

He is a confirmed member of the Household of the Prophet (follows the Sunnah) from anywhere in the world and follows the Holy Qur'an and the Way of the Prophet.

He is admired by all because of his attributes and actions all stemming from the fact that he is on a mission from Allah

He has a strong unique personality - he instills the fear and admiration of Allah through his words and actions.

He is intelligent, sharp and well-educated in Islam and in modern standards: The Prophet (pbuh) said 'God has created nothing more noble than intelligence.'

He has a good general knowledge of the world and its peoples.

He has a good public and private image, which must be well-substantiated.

He is a handsome man, in excellent physical and mental health, photogenic and can interact easily with the media: The Prophet (pbuh) said 'Allah is Beautiful and He loves beauty.'

He utilises the latest technology for the aid of Muslims.

He interacts with a proportion of the elite of Muslims, non-Muslims and the masses - in fact, he has encountered all sectors of society

He does not live extravagantly - however, he must portray a good image of Islam in all respects and at all times humanly possible. He is generous but not foolish.

He must have a group of elite Muslims who help him in his work - the best scholars working for him.

A cult of personality will not be built around the leader.

His successor has already been chosen by Allah, and his successor will have the support of all the Muslims of this Earth.

His character is similar to that of Muhammad (pbuh), his attributes and his style.

No factionalism will be tolerated, and nor will any threat to Islam, internally or externally.

He will be THE dominant player on the world stage.

The principles of Islam and the love and fear of Allah will always come first.

He will create a global Islamic state, not a country filled with Muslims whose leadership only uses Islam in its policies to appease the masses, but hardly ever delivers on them. To understand the role of the Islamic State, here is its Constitution:

The Islamic State

The Constitution of any Islamic State-

1. The Holy Qur'an.

2. The Authentic Sayings and Traditions of Prophet Muhammad (pbuh).

3. The Decisions of the Four Pious Caliphs which are in the light, spirit and conformity with the Holy Qur'an and the Authentic Sayings and Traditions of the Holy Prophet

4. Research work (*Ijtihad*) carried out by renowned scholars in the light, spirit and conformity with the Holy Qur'an, the Authentic Sayings and Traditions of the Holy Prophet (pbuh) and the Decisions of the Four Pious Caliphs.

5. Research work (*Ijtihad*) in the process of being carried out by contemporary renowned scholars in the light, spirit and conformity with the Holy Qur'an, the Authentic Sayings and Traditions of the Holy Prophet (pbuh), the Decisions of the Four Pious Caliphs and the Research Work (*Ijtihad*) of the renowned scholars in the past.

6. By Consensus (*Ijma*) reflecting the essence and spirit of the Holy Qur'an, which is to be ratified by a broad-based panel of scholars of knowledge. And finally, to be confirmed by the Head of the Islamic State.

7. The Holy Qur'an.

8. The Holy Qur'an

9. And The Holy Qur'an.

THE SITUATION BEFORE HE COMES - SOUND FAMILIAR?

The Prophet (pbuh) stated in the seventh century
that this would be the situation before the arrival of the Mahdi.
These are the extrapolations for his hadith.
All Praise to Allah - how right he was.

- *There will be many reciters but few men of real knowledge.*
- *Usury will be widespread – no will be able to escape usury.*
- *There will be lack of trustworthiness between people, when authority is given to others than those who deserve it.*
- *The True Muslim will be attacked and vilified by Muslims and non-Muslims for promoting the right and forbidding the wrong. He will be a stranger amongst his own people.*
- *When the Arabs are abased, Islam will be abased.*
- *There will be a refusal to rule and judge by the Revelations of Allah.*
- *There will be many skyscrapers, time will shorten and slip away, and there will be many earthquakes.*
- *The Muslims will imitate the non-Muslims.*
- *There will be women who are barely wearing any clothes in public.*
- *War aeroplanes whose sound will terrify the Muslims because they bring death and destruction.*
- *There will be recording machines and spy devices abound, when man can be traced anywhere he is in the world.*
- *The men of real knowledge will be eliminated.*
- *The good qualities of the Europeans makes them the dominant force on Earth.*
- *The wicked will have a say in public affairs, the liars wil! be believed and those without nobility and those without nobility and honour will be triumphant.*
- *The unbelievers and those of the disbelieving sects will be reciting the Holy Qur'an.*
- *There will be reversion to idolatry – cult of personalities and the worship of the evil dictator.*
- *There will be an abundance of wealth and women.*
- *Increasingly people will desire death.*
- *Allah will cause earthquakes because of fornication, alcohol consumption and sexual music and there will be fornication and nudity in public.*
- *There will be insincerity in the Hajj.*

Each one of these has been fulfilled - anytime until Allah's Command.
But only if a Muslim acts as a Muslim and unites with his fellow Muslims around the globe.

THE MAHDI

By the Grace of Allah, the Almighty, this man is going to save the World.

No man, no law, no war can stop him.

He will establish JUSTICE on this Earth

He will fulfill his mission - ALLAH WILLS IT SO

He is coming.

HIS BLOOD IS THAT OF THE PROPHET MUHAMMAD (PBUH)

He *is* a descendant of the Prophet Muhammad (pbuh)
through his daughter Fatima (may Allah be pleased with her).

The Prophet (pbuh) said **'The Mahdi will be one of my descendants, from the children of Fatima.'**

HIS NAME - THE PRAISED ONE

The Prophet (pbuh) said **'The world will not pass away before the Arabs are ruled by a man whose name will be the same/ resemble my name.'**

His name could have a similar meaning as the Prophet (pbuh) **- The Praised One**
His name could contain the root ***Hah, nun, dhel*** **- Muhammad, Ahmed**
He could have one of the many names which the Prophet (pbuh) has been given.
His father's name could contain ***'Abd'*** **- like the father of the Prophet (pbuh) called Abdullah**

THE BRAVE & ADMIRABLE KING GUIDED BY ALLAH

The Prophet (pbuh) said
'There have been four great kings on the Earth: two were believers and two unbelievers.
The believers were Dhu'l-Qarnayn and Sulayman, and the unbelievers were Nimrod and Bakhtinasr.
There will be a fifth king, from the people of my household.'

The Prophet (pbuh) said 'The Mahdi is the peacock of the people of the Garden.'

HIS APPEARANCE

The Prophet (pbuh) said: 'The Mahdi will be of my stock,
and will have a noble forehead and a high, prominent nose.'

THE RIGHT MAN AT THE RIGHT PLACE AT THE RIGHT TIME

He will emerge and rally his forces to help the community to remove their distress, thorough his sincere desire to rid the lands from the domination of the impious, sinful people who rule them. He will defend all righteous people against the unbelievers and tyrants. His troops will be victorious and the people of the heavens and Earth, birds and wild animals will rejoice in his rule.

THE NIGHT HE EMERGES

The Prophet (pbuh) said 'The Mahdi is one of us, from the people of my household.
Overnight, Allah will inspire him and prepare him to carry out his mission successfully.'

THE MAN WHO SPEAKS WITH THE PROPHET'S (PBUH) SUNNAH

The Prophet (pbuh) said 'A man from my nation will come who speaks with **my Sunnah** and Allah, the Mighty, the Glorified will send showers of rain from the heavens so that the Earth will produce from its blessings.

HIS BIRTHPLACE - MEDINA

Imam Ali (may Allah be pleased with him) said 'The birthplace of the Mahdi will be in **Medina.'**

THE HAPPIEST TIME ON EARTH FOR THIS UMMAH

The Prophet (pbuh) said 'During the last days of my community, the Mahdi will emerge.
Allah will give him abundant rain and the Earth will bring forth its crops

and give forth its wealth and herds will multiply and the community will be huge.'

THE INVINCIBLE CHAIN OF THE CHOSEN LEADERS

The Prophet (pbuh) said 'A nation which has me at its beginning, 'Isa ibn Maryam at its end and the Mahdi in between will never be destroyed.'

JUSTICE AND HAPPINESS- THE ISLAMIC WAY

The Prophet (pbuh) said 'The Last Hour will not come until the Earth is filled with injustice and oppression. Then a man of my family (or of the people of my house) will emerge and fill it justice and equity as it was previously filled with injustice and oppression.'

The Prophet (pbuh) said 'The Mahdi will remain in my community for at least seven, eight or nine years. In those years, my community will enjoy a time of happiness such as they have never experienced before. Heaven will send down rain upon them in torrents, the Earth will not withhold any of its plants, and wealth will be available to all. A man will stand and say, "Give to me, Mahdi!" and he will say, "Take."'

The Prophet (pbuh) said 'Allah will send a man from my family and he will fill the Earth with justice and equity as it was previously filled with injustice and tyranny. The inhabitants of the heavens and the inhabitants of the Earth will be pleased with him and such plants will be produced by the Earth that the living will wish the dead could come back to life (when they see the happiness and blessing of the Earth and the might of Islam.)'

THE GREATEST VICTORY

The Prophet (pbuh) said 'Woe to this community from tyrannical rulers! How they kill and terrorise God-fearing people, except for those who appear to obey them! Some God-fearing believers will pretend to co-operate with them with their tongues but flee from them in their hearts. When Allah Almighty wants to restore the power of Islam, he will crush every stubborn tyrant. He has the power to do whatever He wishes to put the community right after its corruption.....if there only remained a single day of the this world, Allah would lengthen that day until a man from the people of my house was given control over it.
Battles will take place under his command and Islam will be victorious.
Allah does not break His promise and He is the Swift-Reckoner.'

THE RIGHTEOUS NEVER GIVE UP THE CHASE

The Prophet (pbuh) said 'A group of my community will continue to fight for the Truth and overcome those who resist them until the last of them fights the False Messiah.'

THE EVENTS

Halley's Comet will come during the lifetime of the Mahdi.

HE NEVER TAKES THE POWER - HE IS GIVEN POWER BY THE PEOPLE

People will come to him and they will FORCE him to accept their allegiance.

WHO & WHEN: ONLY WHEN THE MUSLIMS ACT WILL ALLAH SEND HIM

The Prophet (pbuh) said
'If there were only a single day of this world left, Allah would lengthen it until He sent a man from me or my family whose name is my name and whose father's name is my father's name.'

ALLAH
WILL LENGTHEN TIME
UNTIL THE MUSLIMS ACT AS MUSLIMS
AND UNITE

THE EMERGENCE
The Mahdi is coming, if he is not already here.

THE RIGHTEOUS
You will believe that a man can be righteous.

THE PREPARATION
You must prepare for his arrival.

THE ACTION
He is a man of action.

THE BRAVERY
There is none we have seen who will be so brave
who will eliminate injustice without any fear
for it is Allah Who gives him the strength and bravery

HE IS A MAN OF TRUTH
There is Divine Substance in his words

YOU WILL KNOW HIM
There can only be One

TIME'S UP
Those who do not believe are trembling

THE RELENTLESS PURSUIT
Once he begins the Chase, he will never stop -
He will strike down on the Enemies of Islam like lightning in the monsoons

In the Dark of Night,
Abound the Chariot of the Righteous,

A Saviour will emerge
To wipe out every injustice

Whom The People will call
The Mahdi

ALL PRAISE IS DUE TO ALLAH,
THE LORD OF THE WORLDS

THE KINGDOM OF ALLAH

'Blessed is He in Whose Hand is the Kingdom; and He is Able to do all things.'
(HQ, 67:1)

THE MUSLIM NATIONS OF TODAY: THE ISLAMIC WORLD OF TOMORROW

Your Leader will then form an organisation which every Muslim leader in the world will accept and so will every Muslim. Every other Community around the world will admire, love, respect and fear the words and actions of this entity.

IF ALLAH WILLS

It will be the Islamic State
It will be the Kingdom of Allah
Its Leader will be the Mahdi
It will have the Mahdi's Commanders in each land
It will be governed by the Constitution of the Islamic State
The Prophet Jesus (pbuh) will lead this entity after the Mahdi
It is the Millennium that will cause the ISLAMIC EVOLUTION.

'The Master of the Day of Judgment.' (HQ, 1:4)

Globalisation: Power in the Wrong Hands

'Globalisation is a euphemism for 'transnationalisation' - the unfettered expansion of transnational corporation into the world economy, particularly into the economies of the poor countries. The multilateral organisations such as the World Trade Organisation, the IMF and the World Bank are playing a key role in this process.'

The world is now a 'global village'. This has come about as a result of the inventions made by the West in the last two centuries, which were basically innovations from what the Muslims had spent a thousand years inventing. The steam train, the steamship, the car and the aeroplane have greatly speeded up the transport of people and goods around the world. Telephones, radios and all kinds of electronic media have accelerated the communication of ideas and commands to an extraordinary level and television and improvements in newspaper productions mean that what is regarded as news reaches ordinary people in every part of the world almost immediately. The Internet means people can speak, listen and interact with each other whether they are in Chile or in Siberia. Communication, Planning and Execution is almost Instant.

The technological innovations and industrial developments have had many important results. One is the unification of the world, or globalisation to create a New World Order. This is seen in the unification of the United Nations. The most it provides is a forum in which representatives of nearly all the inhabitants of the world can express their views. The ease and rapidity of travel allows political leaders to regular meeting their counterparts from the remotest parts of the world.

However, unification depends on the people who are being united, and this unification of belief does not exist.

The main belief should be 'Peace to all Mankind', but this century has been the most bloody and murderous in history.

The United Nations: A Failure

'The United Nations organisation is over 50 years old, but still has not proved entirely effective as a moderating agency of international relations. Its faults and flaws are shared by the global community it is a part of, and particularly of its most influential members, the members of the Security Council.'

The United Nations is a failure. Its confused infrastructure is weak because bureaucracy over nation states has meant that global problems could not be solved. Politically, Muslim states have become members of the United Nations, even though some of them feel that it is little more that a tool of Western interests, which it largely is, and that is why change must and will occur immediately.

For example, rather than being a united workforce in solving the world's problems, their objectives have been confused by bureaucracy and also because nation states with widely differing agendas hindered the process. The United Nations fails because the power there is in the wrong hands of the corrupt and the criminals, and also because those who should have power do not have it.

'In their hearts is a disease and Allah has increased their diseases.
A painful torment is theirs because they used to tell lies.
And when it is said to them: "Do not make mischief on the earth,"
They say: "**We are only peace-makers.**"' (HQ, 2:10)

Any measure of success must be measured by an objective - the United Nations was designed to keep the world free of war and tension, which it has not done, because the last century had been the most bloody and violent in all of history so far. It has been unsuccessful in its main aim - to create and sustain world peace.

Additionally, the people who compromise it have either agreed with its policies, and therefore do not believe in global justice, or complained about how ineffectual it really is. Of the problems which involved Muslims, some have been unsolved for decades and criminals left unpunished.

The United Nations must and will receive a major renovation of its infrastructure and a simplification of its organisational structure. Internal voting must be modified, especially with regards to the Security Council, where the equality of mankind is violated through the mechanism of 'Veto' and where the non-Muslims decide the fate of the Islamic world. The present situation is unacceptable.

Many believe that the Muslims, comprising one-fourth of humanity with a global presence and reach, should have a collective permanent seat in the United Nations Security Council.

Do not beg at the door of someone who will not feed you.

Rather, the most important objective the Muslims should have is uniting themselves - if they have any sense, that is when the United Nations Security Council will humbly send an invitation asking the Islamic World to actually govern the entire Earth.

United States & Kingdoms

The United States of America was perhaps the first step in realising that one continent can be ruled by one government and one ruler, The President, with great success in terms of prosperity, because they took the Islamic concept of one continent with one set of beliefs, one ruler and it has worked to an extent. On the other hand, the United Socialist States of Russia was another United States which failed, but this was largely due to the lack of the Communist ideology to accept the concept of The Creator, and so He brought them down. The United Arab Emirates have a successful system, which can be globally expanded to the Islamic world, so that each nation state is an Emirate.

Federalism

The European Union has one Parliament, one currency, one policy - it will work together with the United States of America in mutual confidence to govern the world. However, the thought of the European Union is based on the mere fact that these countries are on the same continent and are geographically close. However, the European Union is made of many differing nations who keep their prejudices to this very day, and this is where both World Wars began. The European Union is a collective of power and resources, but the policies of the nations that comprise it mean that it will have a weak base. That is unless the European Union becomes part of the Islamic world.

The Players

Russia, China, Canada, and India would be blocs, but Islam would have to play a role in these countries as it is doing, so that the bullying which the United States and Europe have sometimes assumed, does not continue. Each of these is an Ummah (community), and one community should not dominate another, be they Muslim, Christian, Hindu, Buddhist, Jew or any other religion.

The Cause of their Decline

However, all these nations which do not have Islam as their official and only policy, have naturally had problems and will have problems until Islam gives the right direction to the region.

a) The rich are getting richer and the poor are getting poorer.
b) Mankind is becoming more liberal in their beliefs- eventually this would mean 6 billion nation states.
c) Lack of unity in belief has meant weakness in effective government.

Thus, those who believe in Allah and are hopeful and optimistic about the future, will realise that any of these blocs who do not have Islam as their main ideology, will indeed be less prosperous, less equipped, less knowledgeable and less strong than the Future Islamic State which the Guided Leader will preside over, if Allah wills.

Organisation of Islamic Conference

Muslim countries came together as a single international bloc at the Organisation of Islamic Conference (OIC). The Organisation of Islamic Conference was set up at the initiative of King Faisal of Saudi Arabia in September 1969. King Faisal called a summit of heads of state of Muslim countries as a result of the incident of arson at the al-Aqsa mosque in Jerusalem that year. The Summit established a permanent secretariat in Jeddah to co-ordinate activities of Muslim countries. Additionally, King Faisal was offered the title of *khalifah* at the Second Summit in 1974, but this was unsuccessful - King Faisal knew that the only *khalifah* was going to be the Mahdi.

The Organisation has three principle organs:
1 - The Islamic Summit of the Heads of the Muslim States which members every three years to discuss major issues facing the Muslim world.
2 - The Conference of Foreign Ministers which meets yearly to implement general policy and review progress on resolutions.
3 - The General Secretariat which promotes co-operation and co-ordinates activities between Muslim countries.

Numerous institutions function under the umbrella of OIC, including the Islamic Development Bank which finance projects throughout the Muslim world, the Red Crescent, the Islamic Science Foundation, the Islamic Centre for Development and Trade and Islamic Relief Agency.

The OIC has developed joint Muslim stands on a number of political issues, such as support for the people of Palestine, oppressed Muslim minorities as well as a number of Third World movements and issues. It has had some success in promoting economic and cultural co-operation between Muslim states and settling disputes between Muslim countries.

'And among His Signs
is the creation of the heavens and the earth
and the difference of your languages and colours.
Verily, in that, are indeed signs for men of sound knowledge.'
(HQ, 30:22)

THE MISSION: **MILLENNIUM ISLAM**

The 'Organisation of Islamic Conference' has name which does not stress the roles Muslims play, nor have many Muslim heard of it or its activities. It is barely existing and has a few institutions which are working for the good of the Muslim world, but not enough is being done. This is a body with not much muscle - it is rather like a skeleton, clinging on to life. This is how it will be given life - THROUGH KNOWLEDGE AND IDEAS.

1) We need to practice and believe in True Islam. The world will realise the Truth of this religion when we project Islam as a religion and a way of life that preaches, peace, harmony, optimism, tolerance, human dignity, and the moral and material prosperity of the world.

2) Each community around the world must try and do this. Pick a man who is your most righteous, trustworthy man and make him your leader. Then he will choose others to fill these people on the basis of piety and merit.

3) The most righteous and trustworthy people should be chosen for each position. The Muslims of the town must choose a Town Commander - who is the most able, trustworthy man who has shown that he can command the respect of the town and has a well-established proven reputation for being honest and trustworthy. This is the prime attribute which you will identify them by. He will then through a process of consultation with righteous Muslims of all ages appoint for his town Muslims in the fields of education, commerce and economics, tourism, public affairs, general infrastructure like police and hospitals, etc. If there are people already in this position, it is for the Town Commander and his immediate council to decide whether they are trustworthy and righteous through their actions, words and deeds. He will fulfill the basic needs of the town through the Islamic Missions Guide and make the pursuit of knowledge and the result of justice key to the town.

4) All the commanders of the towns will meet and elect similar positions on a state/ region/ county/ province level.

5) All the province/ county/ regional commanders will meet and then elect similar positions on a national level.

6) All these national leaders will meet and rule by council until the Mahdi comes.

The Prophet (pbuh) said
'A Muslim is the brother of a Muslim, he does not wrong him, fail to assist him, lie to him or despise him.'

'O mankind!
We have created you from a male and a female,
and made you into nations and tribes, that you may know one another.
Verily, the most honourable of you with Allah is that who has piety and loved good deeds.
Indeed, Allah is All-Knowing, All-Aware.'
(HQ, 49:13)

THE FUTURE ISLAMIC STATE: QUALITIES

These are the attributes that we want the Islamic State to have and this is what our optimistic and realistic targets are. If your state at present does not match this, then change it to suit these policies.

Life can be this good

Head of state and government	Commander of the faithful
Political system	Islam
Administration divisions	Number of boroughs, provinces, states
Armed forces	Core unit in each country
Military Training	Each citizen must be skilled in sports.
Death Penalty	Will be retained and used for serious crimes, acts as a deterrent primarily
Education spending	Priority
Health spending	Priority
Defense	Increased collectively
Currency	Islamic Dinar in that region
Foreign debt	Non-existent
Major trading partners	The Islamic World and the Allies at Peace
Resources	Every
Industries	Every
Imports	Small, minute
Exports	Huge, but only to the Allies at Peace
Population	It is Allah's will
Population growth rate	It is Allah's will
Age distribution	Balanced
Religion	Islam main, with other Ummahs allowed
Languages	The national (not imperialist) language and Qur'anic Arabic
Education (compulsory years)	from birth to death
Literacy rate	100%, Men 100%, Women 100%
Labour Force	Demand is the same as supply, all adults part of labour forc employed
Employment:	100%
Poverty:	0%
Life expectancy	Allah's will, should increase
Physicians	1 per 100 people minimum
Birth Rate	Praise be to Allah, as high as He desires
Child mortality rate	Praise be to Allah, as low as He desires
Death rate	Increased
Marriage Rate:	Decreased
Divorce Rate:	Decreased through health and medicine
Refugees:	Islamic State is a sanctuary

Iqbal Shah said:
'It is in Islam and not in the United Nations that the world,
has realised the brotherhood of man
In the mosque, a beggar and king may stand together in a row,
toe-to-toe, shoulder-to shoulder, and pray to Allah as brothers.
The house of prayer is free to all at any time, and is so that a man may take refuge there
without fear of being injured by his enemy within its precincts.'

'The King of Mankind.' (HQ, 114:2)

THE SPHERE OF JUSTICE

'O you who believe! Stand out firmly for justice,
even though it be against yourself
or your parents or your kin, be he rich or poor.' (HQ, 4:135)

GOOD TRIUMPHS OVER EVIL

'The Prophet (pbuh) said
'Whoever of you sees something objectionable, then let him change it with his hand,
and if he is not able, then with his tongue,
and if he is not able, then with his heart, and that is the weakest faith.'

The Islamic Law of the Millennium is the one that Allah has sent down to the Prophet Muhammad in His Book, the Holy Qur'an and the Sunnah of the Prophet (pbuh). It was practiced for a while many centuries ago, but today only remnants of it remain. All Muslims should see it as a Divine Law which is IDEAL and REALISTIC in this world. This is what the Islamic Law of the Past, Present and Future is, was and always has been. It returns NOW.

ISLAMIC LAW: The Law of Islam as embodied in the Holy Qur'an and Sunnah = *Shariah*
Shariah is the code of law for the Islamic way of life which Allah has revealed for mankind and commanded us to follow. The word Shariah means the clear, straight path or example. It prescribes a complete set of laws for the guidance of mankind so that Good (*Ma'ruf*) will triumph and Evil disappears from society. It provides the CLEAR AND STRAIGHT PATH which leads to progress and fulfillment in life and attainment of Allah's pleasure. The scholars and experts on Islamic Law have made Shariah easier to understand and practice by the science of Fiqh, which is the explanation of the Islamic laws based on the Qur'an and the Sunnah.

Science of Islamic Jurisprudence = *Fiqh.*
It compromises the principles of Islamic laws and the practical injunctions that follow there from.

i) The five basic duties of Muslims in worship towards Allah (*Ibadat)*
ii) The relations of Muslims between Muslims - involving the laws of marriage, inheritance, contracts, divorce, etc. (*Mu'alamat)*
iii) Punishment of Muslims and non-Muslims who commit crimes - (*Uqubat)*

Some great Muslims devoted themselves to the task of developing the science of understanding Islamic law and its practice. The four best known-compilers of Fiqh are Imam Abu Hanifa, Imam Malik, Imam Shaf'i and Imam Abu Hanbal.

Islamic law divides human activities into
1) Duty/ Obligatory (*Fard/ Wajib*) performance of these actions is rewarded and their omission is punished.
2) Recommended (*Mandub*) - actions the performance of which is rewarded but omission of which is not punished.
3) Silent (*Mubah)* - actions permitted by silence.
4) Disliked (*Makruh)* - actions disapproved of but not punishable.
5) Forbidden (*Haraam)* - actions punishable by law.

Shariah is the means to arrive at the ideal life recommended by Islam and enables us to bring our life in line with the will of Allah.

<u>The Instruments of Islamic Jurisprudence</u> (*Usul al-Fiqh*)

The Main Sources of Islamic Law
1. The Holy Qur'an
2. The Sunnah of Prophet Muhammad (pbuh)

The Holy Qur'an is the main source of the Shariah. It states the principles while the Sunnah of the Prophet (pbuh) provides the details of their application. For example, the Holy Qur'an says: establish Salah, observe Sawm, pay Zakah, take decisions by consultation, do not earn or spend in wrong ways - but it does not describe how to do these things. It is the Sunnah of the Prophet (pbuh) which gives us the details.

The Sunnah of the Prophet (pbuh) is the collection of authentic sayings, practices and actions called hadith. These hadith have been carefully collected and compiled since the death of the Prophet (pbuh). Six collections of hadith are regarded as the most authentic. They are Sahih Al-Bukhari, Sahih Muslim, Sunan Abu Dawud, Sunan Ibn Majah, Jami' At-Tirmidhi and Sunan An-Nasa'i. In addition to this, the Muwatta' of Imam Malik, Mishkat Al-Masabih of Abu Muhammad al-Husain bin Mas'ud and Musnad of Ahmad bin Hanbal are also well-known.

Methodological Roots of Islamic Law
3. Consensus (*Ijma*)
4. Analogical Reasoning (*Qiyas*)

Consensus is Ijma and applies to a situation where no clear conclusion can be made from the Holy Qur'an and the Sunnah. In this situation the representatives of the people who are well-versed in the Holy Qur'an and the Sunnah will sit together and work out an agreed formula to solve the particular problem. Ijma developed during the period of The Caliphs who Took the Straight Path.

A reference or analogy or a comparison of one thing with a similar one is Qiyas. It is applied in circumstances where guidance from the Holy Qur'an and the Sunnah is not directly available. A solution to a problem is reached by a process of deduction from a comparison with a similar situation in the past.

MILLENNIUM ISLAMIC LAW: THE SOLUTION

Dynamism is an essential component in Islamic Law - as time moves on, Shariah moves on with it. The principles of Islam as shown in the Holy Qur'an and the Sunnah of the Prophet remain the same, but scholars must apply these sources to every new situation that arises. For example, the Shariah is so complete in that it can describe how best one should dress in all time and ages, and yet have Islamic legislation for nanotechnology, robotics, the Internet, mobile-telephones, bionic technology - everything.

It appears that there are powers which have deliberately tried to stop these scholars from progressing. This is why the position of these scholars in society had fallen, and only a few Islamic Scholars were left. However, the numbers are increasing, all Praise to Allah.

The Islamic Legal Scholar of the Future has to be up to date with the latest technology and the latest trends, so that he and his colleagues can give legal rulings on everything effectively. He must be trained in the Secular Subjects as well as alongside Islam, and he must be at the top of his field in whichever he wishes to specialise. He must remember these words: THE SHARIAH IS ETERNAL AND DYNAMIC

'Indeed, We have sent Our Messengers with clear proofs,
and revealed with them the Scripture and the Balance that mankind may enjoin justice.'
(HQ, 57:25)

THE ISLAMIC COURT OF JUSTICE

The Islamic Court of Justice is to have a global headquarters, and a court in every Islamic nation. Its principle function shall be to ensure that justice is enjoined everywhere on Earth using Islamic law. It shall provide interpretation on various laws passed by the Parliaments so that member states can ensure that decision taken in Islamic National Courts of Justice are in accordance with the International Islamic Court of Justice. It shall provide interpretation on different points of Islamic law, and with regard to the rules and procedures followed by the national courts of justice for their implementation. The appointment of Judges and Law Officials will be on a town, city, state, national, global level.

ISLAMIC LAW ENFORCEMENT

ISLAMIC ZERO TOLERANCE - **Zero Tolerance under the Law of Allah**

Islamic Law in the Millennium is zero tolerance with compassion, which means that NO CRIMES ARE TOLERATED (unless in cases, where compassion is shown to the offender, such as the hungry who steal for food or steal for medicine.)

The Prophet (pbuh) said to a man who entreated him to show mercy on a woman of the tribe of Makhzum who was accused of theft, 'Past nations were ruined because they forgave their nobles when they stole but punished humble men for the same crime.' WE WILL NOT DO THE SAME.

Compassion is the main principle, but only as far as Allah prescribes. If the transgression occurs, it is the duty of the Muslims to be righteous and enforce the punishment at the Command of Allah. This is Islamic Law. It is a law of deterrent. All crimes must be proven in Islamic courts where only the righteous judge and proof beyond a reasonable doubt show that they have committed the act: 'If you anyone kills a human, unless it be for murder or for committing serious crimes in the land, it would be as if he killed the whole of mankind.' (HQ, 5.32)

If you STEAL, you have YOUR HANDS CUT OFF

"As for the thief - male and females, cut off their hands. It is the reward for their own actions and exemplary punishment from Allah. Allah is All-Powerful, All-Wise." (HQ, 5.38)

(Those taking bribes or found of corruption, are seen to have stolen and have their hands cut off.)

This law works on the basis that your two hands are very important tools in your life.

Exceptions: If someone is stealing because they are hungry or very poor, then the law is not implemented, but the offender is employed by the state and is fed and clothed at a decent level.

If you RAPE, you are EMASCULATED and then EXECUTED

Rape is an action largely committed by men against women, but also by men against men. The law prescribes that he who rapes, and is proven to have raped, is emasculated, his property and wealth distributed amongst those he has committed crimes against, and is then executed. Lesson is a deterrent - control is a must, and for those who can no longer exercise control, fast or get married.

If you commit HOMOSEXUALITY once, you are LASHED 100 TIMES. If you re-offend, you are EXECUTED.

Homosexuality is an unnatural crime. The person who commits this crime is lashed 100 times.

If they re-offend, they are executed.

If you commit ADULTERY, you are EXECUTED.

Those who commit adultery and it is proven in the Islamic court are executed. A man can divorce a woman and a woman can divorce a man, so there is no excuse if people find a partner whom they would rather be with.

The UNMARRIED FORNICATORS are to be LASHED 100 TIMES.

'The woman and man guilty of fornication, lash them with a hundred stripes: Let not compassion move you in their case, in a matter prescribed by Allah, if you believe in Allah and the Last Day:
and let a party of the Believers witness their Punishment.' (HQ, 24.2)

If you MURDER, you are EXECUTED unless your victim's family spares you

'O you who believe! The law of equality is prescribed to you in cases of murder:
The free for the free, the slave for the slave, the woman for the woman.' (HQ, 2.178)

Murder, in its greatest degree, those who commit the action and those who organise the crime, are executed and then their property and wealth distributed amongst the murderers' victims' families. If however the victims and families spare the life of the murderer in the Name of Allah, the Almighty, the court agrees to the action.

If you sell or distribute DRUGS, ALCOHOL OR THE DECADENT SEX TRADE, you are EXECUTED.

Those involved in the drugs trade, from the lowest level right to the highest, are executed.

THE SPHERE OF POLITICS

Principles are the basis by which you make, think and act, and therefore these are the basic principles of the political aspect of Islam.

'O mankind!
We have created you from a male and a female, and made you into nations and tribes,
that you may know one another.
Verily, the most honourable of you with Allah is that who has piety and loved good deeds.
Indeed, Allah is All-Knowing, All-Aware.' (HQ, 49:13)

Sovereignty of Allah

Sovereignty means the source of power - in Islam, Allah is the Source of all powers and laws (HQ, 3:154, 12:40, 25:2, 67:1) It is Allah Who knows what is good and what is bad for His Creation. His say is final and mankind cannot change His Law. According to Islam, this order is unchangeable by any parliament or any government which claims itself to be Islamic (HQ, 5:44, 2:229). Laws must be based on the Holy Qur'an and the Sunnah of the Prophet (pbuh).

Vice-regency of Allah - Khilafah of Mankind

Man is the vice-regent or the agent or the representative of Allah on Earth (HQ, 2:30, 6:165). Allah is the Sovereign and man is His representative. Man should do as Allah commands him to do. But he has a choice - either obey or disobey Allah and because of his freedom of choice, he will be tested on the Day of Judgment. In the political sense, *Khilafah* means that mankind would implement the Will of Allah on Earth as His deputy or agent. As Allah's agents, mankind will carry out the Will of Allah on His behalf as a trust (*Amanah*).

Legislation by Consultation (*Shura*)

Islam teaches us to run a government, to make legislation and decisions by the process of *Shura*. *Shura* means to take decision by consultation and participation (HQ, 3:159, 42:38) This is an important part of the Islamic political system. There is no scope for dictators and tyrants in Islam. The Holy Qur'an and the Sunnah will be the basis of legislation in Islam.

Accountability of Government

The Islamic political system makes the ruler and the government responsible firstly to Allah and then to people. The ruler and the government are elected first by the people to exercise powers on their behalf. We must remember here that both the ruler and the ruled are the *Khalifah* of Allah and the ruler shall have to work for the welfare of the people according to the Holy Qur'an and the Sunnah. A ruler is a servant of the people of Islam. Both the ruler and the ruled will appear before Allah and account for their actions on the Day of Judgment. The responsibility of the ruler is heavier than the ruled.

Independence of Judiciary

In the political system, the Judiciary is independent of the Executive. The head of the state or any government minister could be called to the court if necessary. They would be treated no differently from other citizens. The Holy Qur'an has many injunctions about justice. One of the main functions of the Islamic state is to ensure justice to all citizens (HQ, 4:58, 4:1345. 5:8). The ruler and the government has no right to interfere in the system of justice.

Equality before law

The Islamic political system ensures equality of all citizens before the law. It does not recognise any discrimination on the basis of language, colour, territory, sex or descent. Islam recognises the preference of one over the other only on the basis of piety or fear of Allah (Taqwa). One who fears Allah most is the noblest in Islam (HQ, 49:13).

QUALITIES OF THE ISLAMIC STATE

Islamic Territory

The whole cosmos and Earth is the Islamic State. As the Universe expands contracts or decreases, the Islamic state does the same. The whole Earth does not have to be under direct rule of the Islamic state as the rest may yet have to be included - the Islamic state functions and exists regardless.

Citizens of the Islamic State

The citizens of the Islamic State are all those who agree to live under Islamic law. It is every citizen's Guarantor and Protector. If the Islamic state is at a time restricted to a part of the world's population, it does not matter as long as it wills to comprehend mankind. The citizens need not all be Muslims and in fact has hardly ever been all Muslims. The citizens includes all those who AGREE to live under the laws and conditions of the Islamic state because they APPROVE of its order and policies. The Islamic state never binds people to its citizenship against their will. You are always free to move out, together with all their people, relatives, dependents, and everything they possess. These communities can live anywhere in the world, with the Muslims or a thousand miles away. They can live in the desert, in forests, in the mountains, in skyscrapers in cities - it does not matter WHERE they live. If they want to be part of the Islamic State, the Islamic State will protect them.

Muslim Citizens

The Muslims, regardless of their origins, are one Ummah, One Community. We are one entity regulated by Islamic law. The Ummah has its own institutions, courts of law, and schools for the education of its children. We can realise the full measure of our religion, our genius, our ethics and culture - all we have to do is UNITE. The Ummah is then the community living up to our own ideals.

Non-Muslim Citizens

In the Islamic state, there are other communities apart from the Muslim. Each religion has its own Ummah which can live in accordance with its own ethics, culture, language and continue to perpetuate itself in future generations in perfect freedom. The Jews form an Ummah, the Christians form an Ummah, the Hindus form an Ummah, the Buddhists form an Ummah, the Sikhs form an Ummah, the Zoroastrians form an Ummah - indeed, every religion has an Ummah. You do not have to CONVERT to Islam to be part of the Islamic State. Your freedom, your right to your religious identity is guaranteed.

The Islamic state is thus not an exclusively Muslim state, but a federation of Ummahs of different religions, cultures and traditions, committed to live harmoniously and in peace with one another.

The Prophet (pbuh) said

'O people! Surely, your Lord is One, and your father in one.
You belong to Adam (may Allah be pleased with him) and Adam was made of clay.
No Arab is superior to a non-Arab, or vice versa.
No white man is superior to a black man.
Surely, the noblest amongst you are the most God-fearing.'

THE MAIN OBJECTIVES OF THE ISLAMIC STATE

1) MISSION = THE INVITATION TO ISLAM

Mission is certainly endemic to Islam. It flows from its essence as a universal religion. Every Muslim wishes that Islam would be the conscious religion of every person but has been changed by time and culture into something else. The missionary spirit, or *da'wah* (literally, "calling" people to Islam) is the ultimate objective of the Islamic state. Therefore Muslims must carry out the mission both within and outside the Islamic State. Externally, the Islamic State is ideological. It has a world purpose: the extension of itself to envelop the world. It approaches other states, tribes, nations, or groups with the proposal for them to enter an Ummah within the Islamic state. The only results of this entry of another Ummah into an Islamic state means that

a) Its relations with that state will be henceforth be peaceful, that neither state will wage war against the other.
b) A state entering the Islamic state will agree not to live in isolation from the rest of humanity.

2) ADVOCATION OF HUMAN RIGHTS

Under Islam, religious conviction is an entirely personal affair. Each person is free to convince and to be convinced. Unless and until you are convinced of the Islamic claim, you are perfectly entitled to be what you are and to continue to do so from generation to generation. As any Ummah cannot be isolationist, the Islamic State cannot tolerate any encroachment of one Ummah over another. Its duty is the same toward all: to keep the peace, to run the public services, to defend the totality, and to protect the rights and privileges of the persons and their Ummah which constitute the state. Using force or subversion to spread the word of Islam is a punishable criminal violation in Islam. These are the human rights present in the Future Islamic State:

a) There is the security of life and property
b) There is the protection of honour.
c) There is the sanctity and security of private life
d) There is the security of personal freedom
e) There is the right to protest against tyranny
f) There is the freedom of expression
g) There is the freedom of association
h) There is the freedom of conscience and conviction
i) There is the protection of religious sentiments
j) There is the protection from arbitrary imprisonment

3) THE LEGITIMATE USE OF FORCE

Force is not to be in the hands of any Ummah, not even the Islamic Ummah.
Force is in the hands of the Islamic state, or "world order" exclusively.

Its duties:
i) To put down rebellions with any Ummah against its institutions and authority.
ii) To restore to any Ummah the rights, privileges, or properties which any other Ummah might have violated.
iii) To defend the world order itself against its enemies

THIS SYSTEM WORKS

THE GLOBAL MILLENNIUM ISLAMIC STATE

The duty of an Islamic State is to establish *Salah*, *Zakah* and promote the right and forbid the wrong (HQ, 22:41). It is responsible for the welfare of all its citizens - Muslims and non-Muslims and must guarantee the basic necessities to all citizens. All citizens of the Islamic State enjoy freedom of belief, thought, conscience, and speech. Every citizen shall be free to develop his potential, improve his capacity, earn and possess.

The Islamic state is duty-bound to implement the laws of the Holy Qur'an and the Sunnah.
Allah, the Almighty, has denounced those who do not decide their matters by His Revelations.

The Islamic state shall ensure a fair distribution of wealth as Islam does not believe in equal distribution as it is against the law of creation.

Though there are many Muslim countries, there is not a single Islamic state in the world. An Islamic State is based on the model of the Prophet Muhammad's (pbuh) state in Madina while a Muslim state is the one which has a majority Muslim population and some Islamic features.

This all changes with Millennium Islam. The future is when Islamic groups in these Muslim countries and non-Muslim countries belonging to the main group of Muslims work together for the creation of an Islamic State, with the main idea that the Mahdi will be the one who presides over this entity. The work to establish the Islamic State has been done for many years, and the work of the good Muslim never finishes. It is in the coming years of the Millennium that the Islamic State of the Future is coming.

The Islamic State is a world order, with a government, a court, a constitution and an army. To enter it is to decide on peaceful intercourse with one's fellow humans and to renounce war between the Ummahs once and for all. To be outside the Islamic State, means to be isolated, at war and aggressive. The Islamic State is the House of Peace.

The Present:
The New World Order based on terror, on the balance of power, or on the imperial tyranny of any Ummah over the others which is considered by Muslims as satanic.

NOW:
The Kingdom of Allah that Islam envisages is an ideal order of national and international relations where Allah's Law becomes reality.

THE SPHERE OF COMMERCE, ECONOMICS & TRADE

'And the heavens, He has raised it high, and He has set up the Balance
in order that you may not transgress due balance.' (HQ, 55.7-8)

Islam has given us detailed regulations for the conduct of our economic life which concerns mainly the earning and use of wealth. Man needs bread to live but he does not live for bread alone. This means that earning and spending money is essential for our living, but means that we do not live only for this. We have a greater purpose of life. We are Allah's agents on Earth. We not only have a body but we have a soul and conscience as well. Without soul and conscience, we would be considered little more than animals. Everything in Islam is for the benefit and welfare of mankind. The economic principles of Islam aim at establishing a just society wherein every one will behave responsibly and honestly, where there is regard for honesty, truth, decency, trust and responsibility. This is the society which occurs now.

Earning and Expenditure by Halal means

Islam has prescribed laws to regulate earnings and expenditure. Muslims are not allowed to earn and spend in just any way they like - you must follow the rules of the Holy Qur'an and the Sunnah.

1) Any earnings from the production, sale and distribution of alcoholic drink is unlawful, as are earnings from gambling, lotteries and from interest (Riba) transactions. (HQ, 5:90-91, 2:275)
2) Earning by falsehood, deceit, fraud, theft, robbery, and burglary are unlawful. Deceitful acquisition of orphan's property has been particularly banned. (HQ, 2:188, 4:2, 6:152, 7:85, 83:1-5)
3) Hoarding of food stuff and basic necessities, smuggling and artificial creation of shortages are unlawful. (HQ, 3:180, 9:34-35)
4) Earnings from brothels and from such other practices which are harmful to society are also unlawful. (HQ, 24:23).

Islam strikes at the root of evil and wants to establish a just and fair society. A Muslim must earn his living in halal ways and he should always bear in mind that whatever he does, is known to Allah. Extravagance and waste are strongly discouraged (HQ, 7:31, 17:26, 19:27-31, 25:68).

Right to Property and Individual Liberty

Islam allows you to own your earnings. The Islamic State does not interfere with the freedom of speech, work and earnings of an individual provided this freedom is not harmful for the greater good of society. Every individual will be answerable to Allah for his or her actions. (HQ, 4:7, 36:71, 16:111).

System of Compulsory Welfare Contribution (Zakah)

Compulsory payment of Zakah is one of the main principles of an Islamic economy. Every Muslim who owns wealth more than his needs, must pay the fixed rate of Zakah to the Islamic State. Zakah narrows the gap between the rich and the poor as it helps fair distribution of wealth and is a form of social security. The Islamic State is responsible for providing basic necessities of food, clothing, housing, medicine and education to every citizen. No one should have any fear of insecurity or poverty. (HQ, 9:69, 98:5)

Prohibition of Interest (Riba)

An Islamic economy is free of interest. Islam prohibits all transactions involving interest. It allows zero rate of interest. Interest is neither a trade nor a profit. It is a means of exploitation and concentration of wealth.

'They say, trade is like interest and Allah has allowed trade and prohibited interest.'
(HQ, 2:275).

'O you who believe, observe your duty to Allah and give up what remains (due) from interest, if you are believers. But if you do not do it, then take notice of war from Allah and His Messenger; and if you repent, then you shall have capital. Do not exploit and be not exploited.' (HQ, 2:278-279)

Interest is the basis of modern capitalism and is completely opposite to Zakah. Zakah channels wealth from the rich to the poor while interest takes away wealth from the poor and hands it over to the rich.

Law of Inheritance (Mirath)

Islamic law of inheritance is a wonderful system of stopping concentration of wealth. It provides very detailed laws regarding the rights of dependents over the property of the deceased person. 'The Women' (HQ, 4) of the Holy Qur'an deals with the Law of Inheritance in great detail (HQ, 4:7-12, 1:176).

In addition to the above basic principles, Islam has laid down many more rules about economic life. The Islamic State will bring all productive resources into use, including unemployed man-power, water resources and minerals. It will take steps to root out corruption and all harmful pursuits even if they are economically lucrative. Individual freedom may have to be sacrificed for the social good. Islam encourages simplicity, modesty, charity, mutual help, and co-operation. It discourages miserliness, greed, extravagance and unnecessary wastage.

ISLAMIC ECONOMICS IS THE BEST WAY TO ALLOCATE RESOURCES

ELIMINATION OF DEBT

The West has largely made the rest of the world in debt - only 25% of the richest people in the world control 80% of the wealth. At the end of 1996, the total developing countries' debt was a staggering US $2,177 billion. Of this, over US $800 billion is owed by the Islamic world.

The government of these Muslims countries have borrowed unlawful money using interest, which Allah has forbidden, from international financial institutions like the World Bank or the International Monetary Fund which are all backed up 'a sovereign repayment guarantee form the borrowing country' - meaning that once the government takes the debt, the country has to pay the amount borrowed with interest FOREVER. This effectively means that the debt is the obligation of the people, regardless of the fate of the leadership which incurred it. Thus in the case of Zaire, the burden of the US $14 billion debt left by President Mobutu has to be shouldered by the people of that country - the money was corrupt, it was borrowed by the corrupt, used for corrupt means but the debt lies with the innocent poor people.

The people of many developing countries, Muslim or not, are hapless sufferers as the criminal lenders continue to heap mountains of debt on them.

When the Islamic Missions are carried out, someone can declare that the debt was signed illegally - that Muslim people had to pay interest on loans which they never wanted to take. The decision of the Court of Allah is final - the Islamic world does not have to pay any debt on which they have had to incur usury (only pay those which have no usury on them - as if you are exchanging one exact good for another exact good) once they are unified.

All those countries which wish to be part of the Islamic State, but are not Muslims but another community, do not have to pay interest on any loans.

THE UNLAWFUL DEBT IS ILLEGAL - ALLAH AND HIS MESSENGER HAVE MADE THEIR LAW KNOWN.

No Muslim will ever have to take out a loan on interest once there is unity-
for they should heed the warning of the Prophet (pbuh) would have been heeded:
'Usury is equal to seventy sins, the least of which is a man's fornication with his mother.'
'Allah has cursed the consumer, the payer and the recorder of usury and those who refuse to pay zakah.'
In the face of such damnation, you will never incur a debt with interest on it.

ISLAMIC GLOBAL BUSINESS

The Best of Mankind, Muhammad (pbuh) was a Merchant, a Trader, the best salesman in the region who made double the previous sale record for Khadija (may Allah be pleased with her) on his first business trip for her, using his great personality - and we must emulate his style of business. Efficiency, Productivity, Growth and Profit Maximisation can be found in any Economics textbook - 'Islamic Economics' has as its prime concern justice, concern for man and his physical, emotional and spiritual needs and for his environment and surroundings. Your prime motive for business and trading - help your family, help your community, help Muslims, invite non-Muslims to Islam and by doing so you seek to please Allah.

Transnationals - The new international powers

'Transnational corporations are the powerful players in the "global village" beyond the frontiers established in previous centuries by the nation-state. Centralisation of decision making, increasing takeovers and mergers allow them to expand geographically in search of lower production costs and bigger markets.'

Transnationals are going to face the most powerful business competitor in the history of mankind: ISLAM. If they want to have a piece of the Islamic market, they are going to have to abide by Islamic law. That means global halal products, no more sweat-shops, more social justice, more environmentally-friendly products, higher wages on a global scale - we are going to cut into your fat illegal profits and make you pay fairly for the profits you make - no more 'fast bucks'. You will make a profit if you abide by Islamic Law - if you are willing to do this, you are most welcome and we bid you a successful halal mission:

'O you who believe! Eat of the lawful things that We have provided you with and be grateful to Allah, if He is indeed Whom you worship. He has forbidden you only the corpses of animals, and blood and the flesh of swine and that which is slaughtered as a sacrifice for others than Allah.' ' (HQ, 2:172-173)

The speculative economy takes control

'In recent years, 97.5 percent of international monetary transactions were of a speculative nature, that is, money was exchanged for money. The potential consequences threatened global financial agreements, the sovereignty of nation states and the futures of millions of people.'

Gambling, in the form of modern insurance, casinos and speculative economics, is a business. Everyone wants to make a profit. Gambling is illegal in Islam because it is unfair - when a man gambles at a casino and wins, there are a hundred losers who have tried the same gamble and lost. However, that man then tries his luck at the roulette wheel, loses his win, and there are 101 losers. When you buy out an unlawful insurance policy, the aim is to try and make a profit, and if a claim arrives, then to evade paying it through one of the numerous clauses. Insurance is a business, and these criminals will use any unfair measures to make sure that they make that profit. If 97.5% of international monetary transactions are speculative, and not based on good common business sense on what is a good investment and not, is not the international economy inherently weak? One wrong mistake, and the world is in chaos - unless Muslims take control of the economy and build it along the Islamic path. International financial institutions have been gambling with Islamic and non-Islamic money, a very dangerous, illegal and unsound business venture, so Allah wills that the system will collapse. It will make way for the Islamic system which is fair, profitable and based on good old business sense of what is a good halal investment and what is not.

However, the West has already realised that Islamic Banking is the Future - that is why every international business and commerce institution around the world is researching the Islamic way of business: 'The US-based Citibank has become the first Western financial institution to launch a full-scale Islamic banking subsidiary.' Islamic Banking is the Future of Global Business and it is only Muslims who can establish a truly Islamic banking system - you will establish this system.

INTER-ISLAMIC TRADE

The development of Inter-Islamic Trade will unite the Islamic world and bring prosperity to all, not just to the rich. This is how we are going to bridge that gulf.

The current trade figures of 12% for exports and 11% for imports present a rather dismal picture of Inter-Islamic trade. Therefore, an effort must be made by all those Muslims involved in commerce, business, trade and economics to increase the level of Inter-Islamic trade to 100%. This will be done by having one common market for Muslims, the Islamic Common Market and one currency, the Islamic Dinar.

In spite of the phenomenal volume of overall trade carried out by Muslim countries, it is of great importance that the amount of trade that they do with each other is so small. If only these countries formed one market, all their problems would be solved. This is what Muslims must strive for - breaking down those national borders between the countries and regarding them as being just another bridge to your fellow Muslims. The billions of dollars which are traded in imports and exports of fuel, food, primary products, manufactured products, machinery and transport equipment, import of chemicals and textiles should be circulated in the Islamic economy of the world, and will soon measured in the Islamic Dinar. So he who is in Bosnia-Herzgovina should be made to feel at home in Dubai, because both will, in the future, have one market and be part of one entity. Thus, Muslim countries must have one market, one law, and one currency and that is how they will be prosperous.

ISLAMIC TRADE ORGANISATION

Islam is against the imposition of customs, maintaining that a country that levies customs is inhibiting the free distribution of wealth around the world and is encouraging a type of industry or agriculture for which it is not suited. A free worldwide distribution of wealth and goods, however, would only be effective with a free worldwide distribution of layout.

Indeed, it would be an Islamic desire to dispense with all customs and immigration institutions. Men and women ought to be free to live and produce halal wealth wherever they wish without checks and hindrances.

The aim of the Islamic Development Organisation is to incorporate the development of the Islamic world into a set of policies to develop their economies using these principles. The organisation should have an office in the commercial capital of every country in every Islamic world, and some in non-Muslim countries. Additionally, each town, province and state must have their own employee of the Islamic Development Organisation, so that the grass roots of Islamic society are playing as much of a part in the process of the development of the Islamic world as those businessmen, economists and academics who are forming the policies. This will mean the collection and processing of information, planning and then appropriate policy in the Departments of Industries, Agriculture and Infrastructure in all Muslim communities will occur, with a view to development to the highest degree and for all Muslims.

In the Department of Industry, the entire resource base of the Islamic world will be converted into viable industrial projects with the best Muslim minds behind its development. In the Department of Agriculture, all food and development will be increased to meet levels of health in all Muslim countries, with priorities given to those Muslim countries suffering from starvation and inadequate supplies and machinery to grow their own food. In the department of infrastructure development, the route of Islamic trade will be streamlined and the development of highly efficient trade routes via air, land, sea and possibly space, as highways and bridges will be made using the latest safety and technology concepts available.

ISLAMIC CHAMBER OF COMMERCE AND INDUSTRY

The Islamic Chamber of Commerce should be set up in every major commercial capital of every Muslim nation to promote the co-operation of trade and investment in every Muslim nation. It will also aim to make non-Muslims see the benefits of halal investment, the dividends of which can be reaped in this world and in the next, if Allah wills.

ISLAMIC COMMON MARKET

The Islamic Common Market will be anywhere on this Earth which wishes to trade under Islamic law, but will begin in Muslim majority countries. However, let us identify the obstacles to this and their solution using J. Siddique's analysis:

SIZE - The Islamic Common Market will compromise the largest single region on Earth, where almost one third of the world's countries are Muslim states. Thus, it will have one Commander, with many governors, each working in union for the glory of Islam. It will be several times larger than the European Common Market in number of consumers and the areas it covers, but its prosperity will be much greater.

DISPARITY- Some may argue that they are too many differences in the levels of income, wealth, resources and state of development that it is difficult for Muslim nations to be integrated under one banner. These people are largely pessimistic whereas a Muslim is always an optimistic realist. The fact that Muslim countries are under one banner will mean that the levels of wealth, income, resources and state of development are evened out to fair levels.

INFRASTRUCTURE & DEVELOPMENT- The basic infrastructure such as roads, highways, air, sea and space transport facilities are not adequately developed for the smooth and efficient transport of goods. However, once the structure of organisations comes in and the wealth is provided, the infrastructure can be developed rapidly.

EXISTING TRADE ALLIANCES AND TREATIES BY MUSLIM COUNTRIES - Some Muslim countries are already members of different trade and common markets agreements signed by them with other Muslim states, or with non-Muslims. However, those trade negotiations made with Muslims are easily incorporated for all will agree to a dissolution of the contract, and immediate entry into the Islamic Common Market. Additionally, contracts and treaties with non-Muslim nations have to be reviewed because often Muslim nations have profited in unlawful means as part of these treaties or they have had to act against their fellow Muslim or they have lost more or being further subordinated as being part of these treaties. Those treaties which have been signed by previous and present governments for the Islamic world must be first reviewed for whether they are binding in all Islamic terms and contain nothing which is unlawful in Islamic law, and then they must decide whether this contract is viable in the wide Islamic Common Market. If it is Islamic, then it remains and will gain more members of the Islamic Common Market.

Islamic Common Market Agreement

1. Free and fair trade throughout the entire Islamic world - no restrictions over regional borders.
2. No taxes, tariffs or duties..
3. Freedom of movement for all citizens to work.
4. Homogeneity of business rights.

Common Market Plan

1. One uniform tax to be placed on everything.
2. The Islamic world removes all quota restrictions on products and services.
3. Common External Tariff for those at peace with the Islamic world.
4. All tariffs on basic materials and food eliminated.
5. Organised barter occurs.

Islamic Common Market Zones

The world will be divided into zones, with geographical location and some similar characteristics as language and resource base being common criteria, but Islam is the primary and most significant criteria. Each Muslim state which is poor in state development will be patronised by at least one Muslim state which is at a higher stage in its development. Thus Muslims will be helping Muslims. This will lead to the biggest economy ever made, with the greatest prosperity, the greatest resources and the greatest people, the Muslims.

ISLAMIC TRADE ORGANISATION

Functions of the organisation to have town/village, city, town/province/state, national and global representation:

1. To work as the principal regulatory body for the Islamic Common Market and streamline basic rules, regulations and procedures necessary for the operation of the Islamic Common Market.
2. To devise and implement the various trade policies including policies on tariffs, duties and procedures of trade etiquette conducting Inter Islamic trade between Muslim states.
3. To perform arbitrary function in settlement of any 'friction' between exuberant Muslim states.

ISLAMIC MONETARY UNION

These are some of the obstacles which some perceive for Islamic Monetary Union and their SOLUTION:

1. Disparity between the level of incomes of various Muslim states
2. Inadequate development of their central banking and monetary systems.
3. Rapid fluctuations on the local currencies in foreign exchange markets throughout the world.

SOLUTION: So what?

The Muslims have the largest single resource base on Earth, they have talent and they are gaining the appropriate education: if they want one currency, THEY CAN HAVE IT. If they want the value of their present currency to be the value of one Islamic Dinar, this can be done. If they want one unit of their currency to be 5 American Dollars by the Will of Allah and through the sustained efforts of the Muslims, IT CAN BE DONE.

The Islamic Dinar: US $5 - this is a generous figure - the true value of the Islamic Dinar is US $5O.

This figure has been worked out using the criteria of natural and diverse wealth of Muslim countries to the United States.

Flotation of Islamic Dinar

Floatation of Islamic Dinar as the common currency of the Islamic World for Inter Islamic Trade, transfer of payments and settlements of accounts will be accomplished through the sustained efforts of Muslims around the world in campaigning and demanding for it. Then it is just a need to get paper together and publish the notes. In each Islamic country, the value of one unit of their currency taken on one day around the world will be taken and then calculated in wealth to an appropriate amount, enlarged in the most poorest countries, and the bank accounts will all be converted and measured in Islamic Dinars. From Albania to Indonesia, the Islamic Dinar will be the only currency. The notes and tenders will be printed under the supervision of the Islamic Development Bank in various styles and colours celebrating the Muslim culture of each state. The Islamic Dinar, the common currency of the Islamic World will be the most stable and powerful currency in the world.

ISLAMIC DEVELOPMENT ORGANISATION

The Islamic Development Bank is considered to be by far the greatest achievement of the Organisation of Islamic Conference so far. Since its establishment in 1976, the Bank has played an important role in financing of Inter Islamic Trade and development projects of the member OIC countries. In every major capital and in every town/ village, there must be Islamic Commercial Banks and Automatic-Teller machines as well as Internet-banking facilities for Muslims. All accounts are in Islamic Dinars, and all banks which are part of the Islamic Development bank as commercial banks, must have their tender changed to Islamic Dinars.

THE SPHERE OF EDUCATION

'Read! In the name of your Lord, Who created. Created man from a clot.'
(HQ, 96:1-2)

The great Islamic centres of learning like al-Azhar University in Cairo, the oldest university in the world, have given way to Oxford, Cambridge, Harvard, Yale, Princeton, MIT, Stanford, Sorbonne, Heidelberg, Tokyo and more non-Muslim institutions. In the Islamic world today, it is the Western education institutes and universities from America, Britain, France and Germany, who with their imperialist past, left an imprint in the minds of the Muslims, that their educational approach is best -Western and often Christian establishments are the premier academic institutions as opposed to the Islamic institutions. In the Islamic world, the study of Islam is seen as being worse in terms of career prospects than something like law, engineering or medicine, and it is seen as being only fit for the 'base' of society or those who could not get into study their primary degrees.

This is a disgrace.

You need to know The Truth

More than half a billion Muslims on this Earth are presently illiterate. This is in sharp and ironic contrast to the first word which Allah revealed to Prophet Muhammad (pbuh): READ.

'So, read as much of the Qur'an as may be easy for you.' (HQ, 73:20)

Only when Muslims learn about their Creator and His Code, and acquire knowledge in His Path, will there be justice. You must follow the religion and acquire knowledge, and then justice will come. That is the only way it has ever come to the Muslims and is the only way it ever will. Thus, all Muslims need to be Muslims and be literate, so that justice can be established on this Earth.

Quality, quantity, and time are key - we need to be have the right education, in the right amount and at a rapid pace. There are certain quarters around the globe who are hostile to the interests of Islam and are contemplating using their knowledge of science, technology, art, literature, military and computers against the largely illiterate Islamic world - their mission is to eliminate us forever. We must be vigilant of these criminal forces, but more importantly, we must equip ourselves effectively through the acquisition of Islam and knowledge.

Western Education - The Best?

That which is currently considered by the majority of the world to be the best education is in the West at establishments such as Harvard, Oxford and Cambridge. It is NOT the best education. Though this education does have its many merits, the flaws are prominent, and like in all things, there is room for improvement. Western education has neglected spiritual and moral imperative in human advancement, and to their full credit, that is why Islam is so widely discussed at their universities. It is the Beautiful Irony of Allah that at these institutions, Islam is so important, whereas themes such as Islamic Jurisprudence are often so looked down upon in the Islamic world as being futile. It is also ironic that those who are currently fighting most effectively in the way of Allah are from some of the highest Western educated backgrounds but are working with their compatriots in the Islamic world. Muslims in the West and all over the world should come to these excellent centres of learning as they have been over the centuries and bring Islam with them, and teach it to the people there in their words and actions. You people are ambassadors of Islam and you need to project the correct images of the true religion.

Islamic Education: Knowledge of the World

On the other hand, let us turn our attention to the Islamic world. Education during Islamic civilisation always carried a strong religious theme. A word for all those money-hungry careerists - the sole aim of education's was never pursuit of a lucrative job - it was the pleasure of Allah and the benefit to the Muslims in all generations. That is how the great scientist such as Ibn Sina, the historians such as Ibn Khaldun, the mathematician and the astronomers, artists, thinkers and architects achieved their status because their works were carried out primarily in the name of Allah and with diligence and patience. Parents were not forcing their children into jobs because of the status that the job would bring - rather it was because the child had God-given talents and if these was honed under the provision of great teachers and a solid infrastructure, the entire world would benefit. These days in the Islamic world, it is only a limited number of jobs which are considered appropriate for students - the whole spectrum of education entails that studying should be enjoyable, and never tedious. Never read because you have to, only read because you want to, and because Allah wants you to.

However, this knowledge must be sought only to establish the Kingdom of Allah on this Earth. Be it space nuclear physics, management or literature, all knowledge must be sought for this sole purpose.

Thus, a plan must be executed in every Muslim community around the world.

Education Objectives

1. *Enhancement of literacy rate of the Muslim populations of the member states to 100%*

Increase the capacity of people to write and read in their own language, and then in Arabic, using the aid of the government from villages to the urban cities and also demanding aid from all the Islamic world, working together to increase knowledge.

2. *Restructuring of education system in every Muslim community around the world by homogenising secular education with religious education at all levels.*

The Curriculum will be based on this essentially throughout the entire world for all Muslims but is flexible provided the system is essentially based on equal footing between Islam and Secular education.

	Secular Education	**Religious Education**
Nursery Level	Making education playful - the child wants to learn and go to school and make friends	Making education as a loving gift from Allah - the child wants to learn, and go to school and make friends
Primary Level	Basic education of social and physical sciences and a vast number of languages - minimum their native language, Arabic and one more language of their choice	Completion of Pure Classical Spoken and Written Qur'anic Arabic, reading and basic understanding of the Qur'an, complete knowledge of basic Islam
Secondary Level	Advance education of social and physical sciences	Optional completion of Understanding and Memorisation of Qur'an. First course scholar, elementary education of Jurisprudence and Hadith
College Level	Graduate and part-time integral employment with a focus in any or all of the social and physical sciences.	Degree of religious scholar, complete knowledge of fiqh, hadith, and shariah.
University Level	Master or Doctorate in social and physical sciences.	Doctorate in specialised subjects, Islamic Law of Jurisprudence or fiqh.

3. *Establishment and promotion of institutions in all fields of academic pursuit, from Commerce to Nuclear Physics.*

At every level, in every community, village/town, city, province/state/county, nation and then on a global level, an Islamic Education Fund must be established, whereby a minimum proportion of Zakah is placed. The rest is tested on the means of the individual, and this is all used for the education of the students in effective ways such as textbooks, libraries, new computers, personal laptops, and more.

In the future, from and during the secondary level onwards, when students have gained adulthood, students will be paid for their education, be given internships and employment in their chosen fields and those which they are most talented for.

History, Economics, Politics, Science, Law, Languages - all these subjects and more have an Islamic component, and it is in the Islamic component that they achieve their best form.

In the educational establishments of the world, in law and in history, in medicine and in art, Muslims are integrating into the university course and environment whilst retaining Islam, showing them to be the best in their fields and starting with the assumption that IT ALL BELONGS AND ENDS WITH ALLAH, THE CREATOR.

This is the advice given by Nik Abdul Aziz with regards to the work of Muslims around the world:

> 'Never stop reading. I read as much as I can, using every opportunity, whether at home, in a car or a plane. Secondly, one must never underrate the experiences of other Islamic leaders and personalities. If it not possible to meet them then one must read their works.'

ISLAMIC EDUCATIONAL, SCIENTIFIC & CULTURAL ORGANISATION

It is the duty of this organisation to acquire more power, which does not come with money, but comes with ideas and concepts. It should implement educational policies along Islamic lines and its presence must be felt on every level - town to globe.

Learning is a journey, not a destination. Education and acquiring knowledge in the service of Allah is a sacred duty imposed on every Muslim. Prophet Muhammad (pbuh) said:

'A believer's belly never becomes full with knowledge;
he keeps on striving until he reaches the end of his life.'

'O My Lord! Increase me in knowledge!'
(HQ, 20:114)

THE SPHERE OF CULTURE

Culture in the future will be very important as will identity. The primary culture of Muslims is Islam and its basic constituents. Upon these are built the smaller cultures of different peoples around the world. Within the larger culture of Islam, Muslims around the world have their own culture for Allah has made Muslims into different tribes and nations, so that we may recognise one another. This mean that you are all Muslims, and within the larger culture of Islam, you should celebrate your own identity as a Muslim from certain parts of the world and also celebrate the culture of your fellow Muslim from other parts of the world. For example, a Muslim in Germany will have certain traditions and customs which have been moulded into the global Islamic culture, and he will share these customs and traditions with a Muslim from Comoros. They will celebrate the diversity of these Muslim cultures and also the unity of the Islamic culture as a whole.

The Spectrum of Islam = **THE UNIVERSAL MUSLIM IDENTITY**

You must get out of the habit of labels. Labels are what irritates a man, especially when the label is wrong. The first and most important label for a person is whether they are a Muslim or not. Nothing else really matters, except for this world. The first question you should ask and be asked is your religion, and your identity is as a Muslim. You have been identified as tribes and nations so that you may recognise one another - but you have allowed your tribes and nations to be the primary aspect of your identity. Your identity is as a Muslim primarily and most importantly - for your main role is to serve Allah and spread the Message of Adam (pbuh) and Muhammad (pbuh). If you are identified as a Muslim, you will be treated as a Muslim. Fellow Muslims will look in admiration at your stance to be identified as one who follows the One True Path of Islam, and non-Muslims will be interested in why you are identifying yourself as a Muslim. Your reply should show them the beauty of Islam. After your introduction, come the labels for this world. Your place of birth, your parents' origins, your ancestry, your regions of origin, your relations, and basically your sense of brotherhood with your fellow man.

Strengths of Muslim and Islamic Culture

Additionally, the strength of some of these Muslim cultures has been so true to the essence of Islam, that the religions and cultures that surround them, have adapted their own religions and cultures more towards Islam. For example, the themes of righteousness, unity, brotherhood, Prophets, and modesty were not present in some cultures. However, when these people encountered Muslims, they changed their cultures, by becoming more righteous, unified, and modest. Indeed, it is not strange to see a religion whose essence was essentially sexual and idolatrous, becoming more inclined towards the values of Islam, when Muslims became part of the community: Hinduism in India has changed itself, especially in the North of India, because of the strength of Islam there. These religions and cultures actually adapted themselves in terms of their basic tenets because the faith and actions of Muslims was so strong, that their message and image was making more and more people embrace Islam, and leave these other religions.

Resistance to unIslamic Culture

However, over time, Muslims from around the world have allowed their culture, and indeed their pre-Islamic culture, to become more important than Islam in their life. They have contributed reprehensible innovations which are contrary to the essence of Islam, through their own concepts, being influenced by their older pre-Islamic customs and also by foreign cultures. Actions considered as FORBIDDEN in Islam are practised in the name of the Islamic culture such as arranged marriages (even though a woman can choose her own husband), female circumcision (a foreign custom) and more despicable actions which are too numerous to mention. Certainly, Muslims have started to act and think in some areas like their non-Muslim counterparts. These non-Muslims resemble them in colour, speak their languages, have similar physical characteristics and some Muslims have forgotten that these attributes count for nothing, when the mindset is different. Though you may look the same and speak the same language, you are totally different, because the Muslim believes in Allah and the non-Muslim does not. The Muslim from Africa more closely resembles a Muslim from China because they essentially believe in the same beliefs and have similar righteous actions and words.

Therefore, these reprehensible innovations into the larger Islamic culture must be removed. Muslims must celebrate their own culture, and where they are from indeed, but always remember that you are part of the larger Islamic culture. Your Muslim culture cannot accommodate the larger Islamic culture, so you must mould your style, traditions and customs into the larger Islamic culture.

TRAVEL AND GEOGRAPHY

'Say:
"Travel in the land and see how Allah and see how Allah originated the creation,
and then Allah will bring forth the creation of the Hereafter.
Verily, Allah is Able to do all things."'
(HQ, 29:20)

Travel today is a thriving business as it was in Islamic civilisation. Muslim ships sailed to every part of the known world whereas many Muslims today are travelling around the world on aeroplanes and jets in search on knowledge, on business and as tourists. Muslim travellers and adventurers were some of the best that the world has ever seen. Sindbad the Sailor and his adventures reflected the realities of commerce and communication during the Abbassid period. The hero of the film, 'The 13th Warrior' (1999), ibn Fadlan was a swashbuckler who encountered amazing dangers and visited far-flung lands such as the Volga-Caspian region in the tenth century which make riveting reading and provide one of the earliest accounts of the areas. Look at the journeys of ibn Battuta (d.1369): 'I visited the lands of every Muslim ruler of my time and travelled to China, Sri Lanka, Byzantium and South Russia.'

Look at those ancient civilisations such as Babylon, the Roman Empire, the Nabateans of Petra, the Pharaohnic dynasties, the Incas, the Aztecs, the Dravidians, the Tang dynasties - with all those ruins and monuments, and realise that they did not listen to the advice of those Prophets (may the peace of Allah be upon them) which Allah sent:

'Say: "Travel in the land and see what was the end of those who rejected Truth."'
(HQ, 6:11)

'Do they not travel in the land, and see what was the end of those before them.
They were superior to them in strength, and they tilled the earth
and populated it in greater numbers than these pagans have done;
and there came to them their Messengers with clear proofs.
Surely, Allah wronged them not, they wronged themselves.'
(HQ, 30:9)

Whether it is by a canoe or by Concorde, whether it is walking or taking space capsules, it is Allah Who allows us to travel:

'He it is Who enables you to travel through land and sea,
till when you are in ships,
and they may sail with them a favourable wind,
and they are glad therein.'
(HQ, 10:22)

Today, Muslims should travel the world, learning the languages and teach Islam to the people of all these cultures. If you live in the South, head North, East and West. If you are in China, head towards Africa. If you are in Pakistan, head towards Brazil. If you are in Germany, head towards Madagascar. Have an exotic adventure and please Allah as well by spreading His Message and appreciating the beauty of His Creation.

'And We placed,
between them and the towns which We had blessed, towns easy to be seen,
and We made the stages of journey between them easy saying:
"Travel in them safely both by night and day."'
(HQ, 34:18)

THE WORLD IS YOUR OYSTER IF YOU HELP TO CREATE **THE KINGDOM OF ALLAH**

'To Allah belong the East and the West, wherever you turn, there is the Face of Allah.
For Allah is All-Embracing, All-Knowing.' (HQ, 2:115)

THE SPHERE OF SCIENCE & TECHNOLOGY

Examples of the Islamic World's Scientific Achievements

Science

Scientific method, as practiced to the present day, was introduced by the great Muslims scientists such as al-Battani (d.829), al-Baruni (d. 1048) and ibn Haytham (d. 1039).

Mathematics

The Muslims turned mathematics into the language of science.
Al-Khwarizmi (d. 850) invented logarithms, algebra, Arabic numerals, concept of zero.
Abdul Wafa (d. 997/8) developed trigonometry, spherical geometry, sine & tangent.
Omar Khayaam (d.1123) solved third and fourth degree equations by intersecting conics - the highest algebraic achievement of modern mathematics.

Astronomy

In his calculation of the length of the solar year, al-Battani was out only by 24 seconds from today's accepted value.
Abdul Wafa discovered variations in the moon's motion.

Optics

Ibn al-Haytham (d. 1039) was the pioneer of optics. Experimenting with 27 different types of spherical lenses, he discovered the laws of reflection and refraction and that the eyes does not send out rays (as Euclid and Ptolemy said) but reflects them.

Chemistry

Al-Majriti (d. 1007) proved the principle of chemical conservation of mass - 900 years later Lavoisier got the credit.

Biology

Al-Jahiz (d. 869) wrote the first comprehensive zoological study.

Physics

Al-Khazini published the 'Book of the Balance of Wisdom' in 1121 containing detailed discussion of measurement and construction of balances, laws of mechanics, hydrostatics and physics, theory of solids, a theory of the behaviour of levers and a theory that identifies a universal central force directed towards the centre of the Earth. Newton's apple would fall 566 years later!

Technology

Muslims discovered the original computers, water power, irrigation methods, surveying techniques, underground mining (complete with miner's lamp) and technologies for manufacturing alloys and steel.

Perhaps the greatest scientific and technological tool of today which has an input in every part of life is the computer.
THE ISLAMIC WORLD INVENTED THE COMPUTER

The first computer

The planispheric astrolabe, the earliest analogue computer is a purely Islamic invention. Made by al-Farazi (d.790 approx.). It was the most powerful tool available to astronomers before the advent of modern instruments With it one could determine the times, setting and culmination of the Sun and stars, and the position of a celestial body at a given time, as well as solve a number of other astronomical problems.

Genetic engineering, bionic technology, cloning, international space stations, the colonisation of Mars and the Moon, hybrids, nanotechnology, artificial intelligence, space lasers, are just a few of the possible realisations which are on the agenda of various governments and individuals around the world.

These are all real and are being researched for this very moment. Just as once upon a time someone invented the wheel to make objects move efficiently, today the reprehensible equivalent of an innovation is someone trying to make men have the babies that women have always had.

Islam has an effect in every sphere of life, as it does in science and technology - however, there must be a point at which morality and science will not meet. For example, is there any point in putting so much money into science and technology when man, woman and child are still starving on Earth? Hybrids of chimps and man are not necessary but some scientists are going to try to achieve this feat, just for the sake of it - that is when science and technology start to become the downfall of humanity.

This is just one way of the ways Muslims can help to use science and technology in the right way, as S. Mahmood explains:

ISLAMIC CYBERSPACE

The Internet allows the exchange of any type of information cross the globe. Photographic quality pictures, sounds, films, can be transmitted around the world. You can access current information, film clips, exchange electronic-mail (e-mail) messages, buy goods, and talk inexpensively through a new Internet phone system. This has become a major tool for learning, education and entertainment.

E-mails enables you to have a personal Internet address and send messages to anyone else in the world of you have their address. The message will arrive much faster than the postal service could deliver and at a fraction of an international telephone call. The World Wide Web is the main system for displaying 'pages' of information, containing easily accessible, text, sound picture and film clips.

For Muslims, the Internet can be a powerful and righteous tool. You can access the Holy Qur'an, hadith, download Islamic Art, and photos of mosques. You can listen to the recitation of the Holy Qur'an and work through Arabic tutorials. You can talk to Muslims from across the world and see them as well. Articles on all aspects of life can be found which will be useful to Muslims - the list is endless.

The Internet is still no substitute for learning Islam directly. The character development and brotherhood achieved when sitting together in circles and spending time in the presence of other Muslims is not possible in front of a keyboard and computer screen. Also, it is not necessarily a good thing for anyone and everyone to be able to instantly access all the Holy Qur'an and hadith references on any particular issue. Without a proper Islamic background, such information can be misunderstood and misused, with harmful consequences.

Widespread distraction of electronic versions of the Qur'an raises the possibility of tampered versions becoming rampant. Anything taken from the Internet, including the Qur'an. It can be altered easily with only a few mouse movements and keyboard taps and redistributed around the world in changed form. Of course, Muslims would not be fooled by this but what about those in the world who have no other proper access to Islamic information? Virtual Islam is not a substitute for interaction between Muslims in the real world.

Those who have the knowledge and facilities will exert greater control over the spread of ideas not necessarily because they are right but because they have the knowledge and technology. In the same way that 'knowledge is power', the ability to control and distribute the methods of information exchange is power.

The jihad today is not just waged on the battlefield. It is also a battle of ideas and a struggle to win peoples' minds. We will not be able to effectively take Islam to the people unless we make good use of the means through which they receive their ideas. So those of us at university, or who have other means of access, should start getting acquainted with what is available and think of ways of developing the possibilities of Muslims in cyberspace. We need to be aware of the dangers we may face and work to ensure Islam is not abused but thrives in this new information age.

It is up to Muslims everywhere to be vigilant and active in making sure that science and technology have their basis as the pleasure of Allah and with a prime aim to establish justice on this Earth. Giant leaps in science and technology are part of Islam, for Muslims were the best at making these giant leaps, but they always kept in mind that science and technology are not something that should be played with, because the effects can be devastating. Therefore, Muslims must make sure that the direction that the leaps and bounds that are made in science and technology are controlled for the sake of morality and the future of humanity.

THE ISLAMIC EDUCATIONAL, SCIENTIFIC & CULTURAL ORGANISATION (ISESCO)

The establishment of the Islamic Educational, Scientific and Educational Organisation is a positive step, but its presence must be stronger and on every level, from the town to the globe. When Islam does eventually reign, science and technology will combine with morality to create the best civilisation the Earth has ever known. It is the duty of Muslims around the globe to be the leaders in solving the problem and making progress for mankind.

Science and Technology - Morality is the Key

'*The relativity of science* - The historical and social relativity of Western science and technology is becoming increasingly reconsidered. Even accepting the usual premise that those are the forces behind progress and wellbeing of the human race, the possibility that they could also become the instrument of their own destruction is becoming difficult to ignore.'

The horrors of science fiction may become science fact, unless science and technology are combined with the Law of Allah.

Industrialisation - Safety is the Key

'*Industrialisation - the magic and danger of plastic* - Plastic had demonstrated very attractive qualities in the age of the technological optimism: adaptability, lightness, flexibility. But with the experience and research of recent years, the undesirable effects are also known: contamination, toxicity, uncontrollable waster and, in packaging, the transference for certain substances to the things contained.'

ISESCO with all Muslims scientists must make sure that plastic and other materials for industrialisation are put under strict scrutiny to make sure they are up to sufficient standards of safety for all mankind.

The Nuclear Force - Harness and Control is the Key

'*Present and future costs* - It will take a Millennium for current levels of toxic nuclear waste to break down naturally, to say nothing of the potential dangers of accidents leaks and nuclear warfare. This means an inevitable toxic legacy for the generations to come.'

ISESCO must make sure that nuclear energy is used for moral means and try to find ways to break down the toxic waste of the criminals' misuse of nuclear energy. The future is Islam, so Allah will help us.

Inventions - Create, in the name of your Lord

Think, plan and create - Muslims must start to invent all goods which are useful for the progress of mankind and submit them to ISESCO for development and production, which will be supported by Islamic wealth. It is through thinking and appropriate planning, execution and distribution that Islam is the future.

How can a religion which was practiced in the seventh century Arabian desert be reconciled with nano- phones, talking computers and planes which carry a thousand people around the Earth? Easy - because the same principles of that age which were applicable in that age, are applicable today and in every age.

The future is Islam where the Word of Allah and His gallant believers is spread across the world in a flash of electricity, where corrupt governments on one side of the world are brought down by the help of believers on the other side of the world, where the man sitting in a skyscraper in Manhattan is reading and believing exactly the same words that the bedouin in a tent in Arabia is - this is a future where Allah's Religion becomes the most powerful scientific and most technologically advanced power on Earth.

THE SPHERE OF ENVIRONMENT

'It is He Who has made you the Agents of the Earth.' (HQ, 6:165)

The Muslims are, by their nature, environmentalists.

As Agents of Allah, Muslims must care for the natural Earth and all it contains. Thus, it was the Muslims who introduced the idea of *hima*, a second kind of inviolate zone, solely for the conservation of wildlife and forests. There were five types of *hima* zone:

1, Reserves in which grazing was prohibited
2. Reserves for forests in which cutting of trees was forbidden
3. Reserves in which grazing was restricted to certain seasons
4. Reserves for bee-keeping in which grazing was forbidden during flowering
5. Reserves managed for the welfare of a particular village, town or tribe.

The principles of these can be easily applied to the modern world - to protect the natural animal and plant life of the planet.

THE CRIMINALS DESTROY THE EARTH

The Earth has been brutalised and scarred. Megatons of toxic waste are now circulating in the oceans, or hovering in the stratosphere. Hormone and plastic pollution has resulted in a 50% drop in male fertility. Every day, another 12 important species become extinct. Every form of life apart from our own, and perhaps domestic animals, have been decimated by the holocaust of modernity. As technology advances, scientific blunders may well wipe out large sections of the human race - that is until you take control through unity.

Biodiversity - The destruction of life

The planet's biological resources, which also encompass their historical, geographical and cultural sustenance, have this century suffered accelerated destruction. This was mainly the work of those who were out just to make a quick buck, and do not care for the costs of society. The righteous of this Earth have been opposing this for decades. The Muslims must protect and monitor the planet's biological resources and not let the criminals get away with stealing them - they are the cause of the depletion in resources and they have been stealing all around the world. This has to stop.

Deforestation - Underlying causes of deforestation And forest degradation

Deforestation rates during the 1980s were as high as 15 million hectares per year for tropical forest alone and the phenomenon accelerated in the following decade in most parts of the world. Forests were not disappearing because people and their governments were ignorant but because a number of interconnected international and national policies prepared the ground for it to happen. These countries' economies have been prosperous for what they have done to the animal and plant life - Allah will give them their just rewards for their unjust actions. Muslims must make sure that they only engage in sensible cutting of trees, because they provide the air that we breathe. By cutting them in huge amounts, these people were trying to suffocate us. Therefore, Muslims for every tree that is cut, a minimum of a greater amount of exactly the same type must be planted in that place.

Climatic Changes - Lack of responsibility or lack of foresight?

Towards the end of the 20th century devastating climatic changes like those caused by the "El-Nino" sea current, or increasing desertfication shows that insufficient action had been taken by the international community to counter the serious problems of human-caused environmental deterioration. The Criminal Man has just worked to gain from this Earth and put nothing back in it - this has led to all sorts of climatic repercussions. These natural disasters which are increasing in strength and volume are responsible for the loss of all types of life. Muslims must lead the formulation of policy to punish any criminal who indulges in activities which have such climatic repercussions. The 1992 Rio Earth Summit revealed that the world is heating up. The industrial gases are turning the planet into a glasshouse, reflecting heat back in rather than out. This has led to increasing desertfication in many parts of the Islamic world - we must unite to stop Muslims dying.

Water - a new source of conflict

Increasingly scarce and vulnerable to destructive human activity, water has become a strategic resource and a determining factor in new conflicts. In the Islamic world, especially in some regions of Africa and the Middle East, conflicts are going to increase between all peoples unless an Islamic Union of Water Supply is created. Drinking water is a basic right, as much as breathing air - when Muslims do not get to drink the water which their Creator has provided for them, the criminals will be given a heavy punishment. All Muslim states must make sure that all Muslims around the world have clean drinkable water.

Demography

The world's population has passed 6 billion. Meanwhile, the debate on demographic growth and the distribution of the Earth's resources which began two centuries ago has not changed. Now is the time for change - Muslims have control of 50% of the world's resources, which they have largely allowed to be sold cheaply to criminal nations, exploited with harmful results, and used them inefficiently. It is a time for change - use your resources well and treat them as if they are on a trust from Allah to you - allocate their use in an Islamically efficient manner.

THE GUARDIANS OF THE EARTH

As the Agents of Allah on this Earth, we cannot standby and let the criminals non-believers destroy our Earth through their pollution, which has led to global warming, ozone-layer depletion and the destruction of plant, animal and human life around the world. We must stop these criminals from polluting our Earth, because if we do not, then this Earth will be destroyed.

'His effort in the land is to make mischief there,
and to destroy the crop and the cattle, and Allah does not like mischief.' (HQ, 2:205)

The Criminals cannot win -
Islam must, and will, emerge victorious.

THE SPHERE OF ARCHITECTURE & INFRASTRUCTURE

'We placed therein broad highways for them to pass through, that they may be guided.'
(HQ, 18:107)

Islamic architecture speaks for itself. Just look at the skyline of Istanbul, the Taj Mahal, Al-Hambra in Granada, the mosque in Cordoba, the Metropolis of Dubai, the Petronas Towers in Malaysia... the list is endless.

A sophisticated science was developed in town planning by Muslims where towns were usually built near a river which supplied drinking and domestic water (upstream) as well as carrying away waste and sewage (downstream and underground). Muslims introduced the idea of carrying capacity and built towns for a calculated number of families. They also introduced the idea of haram - inviolate zones - outside towns, near water courses and other areas - where development was forbidden.

The mosques and colleges were both physically and spiritually at the centre of the town, with the markets (souks) as the centre of commercial and social life. Today, you have the souks as the physical, commercial, social and spiritual centre of life! However, with these measures, the world will have mosques as a focus, an abandon of schools, universities, hospitals, hotels and shopping malls as much as they want - for Islam will return, this is Allah's Promise. The Clause - only if we return as Muslims and unite.

The past, present and future of the Earth can be seen in the architecture and infrastructure of the Islamic world - mosques, schools, universities, homes, gardens, tombs, towers, fortresses, caravans, bridges, hotels, markets, bathhouses, landscapes and more.

THE ARCHITECTURE OF ISLAM

Mosques

The whole Earth has been created as a mosque for man to worship to Allah. However, the mosque as we understand it, is 'jami', the place of congregation and 'masjid', the place of prostration. As the most prominent symbol of Islam because it shows the worship of man before Allah, the mosque has become a worldwide phenomenon. The mosque's main purpose is a place of peace, where one performs ablution, congregates with his fellow Muslims and offers worship to Allah. Muslims have prayed in mosques for centuries. The most religious place on Earth is the Ka'aba in Mecca where millions of Muslims make their umra and hajj pilgrimages. The second most religious place is the Holy Mosque of the Prophet Muhammad in Medina. The third most religious place on Earth is the Dome of the Rock and the Furthest Mosque (Al-Aqsa) which used to be the direction of prayer (*qibla*) before Mecca.

There have been mosques built around the world, in every major city, and in most neighbourhoods in Muslim countries and to an extent in non-Muslim countries. Around the world, these are some of the most famous in the Al-Hambra in Granada, the Al-Azhar Mosque, Cairo, the Blue Mosque, Istanbul, the Friday Mosque, Isfahan, Kalyan Mosque, Bukhara, the Great Mosque, Delhi, and the Great Mosque, Zaire. All Praise to Allah, the list of the Islamic world's mosques, each with its own beauty,

Amongst the most modern are the Mosque of the Islamic Society of North America, Indiana, the Dar al-Islam Mosque, New Mexico, the Taric Islamic Centre, Toronto, the Sherefuddin Mosque, Bosnia-Herzgovina, the Great Mosque, Rome, the Regents Park Mosque, London, the Islamic Centre Mosque, Washington, the Tooba Mosque, Karachi, the King Faisal Mosque, Islamabad, the Great Mosque of Djenne, Mali, the King Abdullah Mosque, Amman, King Hassan II Mosque, Casablanca, the Sultan Omar Al-Saifuddin Mosque, Brunei Darusalaam, the Freedom Mosque, Jakarta - many new mosques are being built as the Muslims return to the mosques all around the world return to Allah.

One can see the beauty of the pure Arabic Qur'an being recited over a cityscape, the blissful echoing voices of a hundred muezzins calling the faithful to prayer. From Damascus to Timbuktu, from Shanghai to Rome, mosques have been built and are being built.

The Collegiate Mosque (Madrasa)
Mosques also used to be the arena in which one acquired an education, and that being knowledge. The learning centre and collegiate mosque (*madrasa*) was an integral part of the mosque, for education was ingrained into worship as it should have been and will be. Discussions would certainly be held on the Islamic religious sciences, but after worship, the mosque would also be host to a multitude of discussions and education of the arts such as architecture, trade, commerce, art, and the sciences such as physics and medicine as can be seen in the case of Ibn Sina in a madrasa in Isfahan. Other famous madrasas include the Mir-I-Aram Madrasa, Bukhara and Al-Muntassir Madrasa, Baghdad amongst many others. Thus, a mosque must also have a library section, though most today have very depleted libraries.

This will change in the future - for us to be the best of mankind, we must acquire knowledge, and books, the written word is what will help us to do this. Therefore, all mosques must start expanding their libraries and computer facilities - they must be a place for knowledge again. More mosques will and are being built, for more Muslims will return to the mosque and make it the centre of their lives. Today, it seems as if the souks and malls are where some people only perform pilgrimage to, as if to pay homage to the material god Mammon who only takes your cash and never gives - but they will and are returning to Allah and to the mosque. This is His Promise.

Universities
There have been many famous Islamic Universities like Al-Azhar, Cairo the oldest university in the world and the Qarawiyyn University, Fez, Aligarh University, India, the International Islamic University, Kuala Lumpur and the Islamic University at Medina. It is no wonder that the American, British, French and German Universities and Institutes are some of the premier academic establishments of the Middle East. It is no doubt that most of the Islamic world which was dominated by an imperial power such as the British or French now have as their premier institutions Christian institutions largely teaching in English and French, and not in the language of the country. The fact of the matter is that Oxford, Cambridge and Harvard were all influenced by Al-Azhar as many spires (minarets) and domes reveal. These universities in the developed world have an architecture which can be incorporated into the wider Islamic culture as will happen.

Homes
Your homes should project the right image of Islam. Whether you live in a house with a courtyard and modern conveniences in the Middle East or you live in a flat in Sydney, Islam should be characteristic of your home. When guests enter, they should realise that Islam plays a role in your life. For example, in the corner of your living room, if you do not have a prayer room, your prayer mat can be found facing Mecca. There may be Islamic calligraphy paintings on your walls. If you have few possessions and are a minimalist, then that is also part of Islam, for it shows modesty and wise spending on your part - no rubbish lying around is very good for a person, whomever they are. Whatever your home is and wherever on this Earth you may live, be it in the desert, the city or in a igloo, the huge spectrum of Islamic culture must be represented in your home, and be dominant over anything else: 'It is Allah who has made your homes places of rest and quiet for you.' (HQ, 16:80)

THE ARCHITECTURE OF THE HEREAFTER

But the architecture of Islam is not just relegated to this world. For example, tombs of some of the great men and women of Islam should be visited such as that of Imam Hussein (may Allah be pleased with him) in Iraq, to offer prayers to Allah for their well-being. However, one must not ask these men for 'assistance' with Allah, as Allah decides our fate in its final determination. Additionally, gardens such as those built in front of the Taj Mahal, India must once again be built because they remind us of the Beauty of Allah on this Earth, and of the Gardens which Allah has mentioned in the Holy Qur'an: 'Verily, those who believe and do righteous deeds, shall have Gardens of Firdaus for their entertainment wherein they dwell forever.' (HQ, 18:107)

THE ARCHITECTURE OF POWER

Military architecture is the most direct expression of power, and the Muslims' power comes from Allah. Gates such as the Gate of Justice in the Al-Hambra, Granada and the Talisman Gate, Baghdad will be built with the emphasis being on admitting the good and excluding the bad. Towers allow the friend to approach and also the identification of the distant enemy, and now are used to how economic might as in the case of the Kuwait Towers, the Petronas Towers in Malaysia, the Emirates Tower in Dubai - but economic might must come second to spiritual strength.

THE INFRASTRUCTURE OF TRADE & TRAVEL

'You shall surely travel from stage to stage.' (HQ, 84:19)

Islamic civilisation has always been mobile. The movement of trade such as the Silk Road, scholars and students going to distant lands to seek knowledge, the transport of goods from one Islamic region to another, emergency supplies in times of disasters, etc. Muslims were very mobile, commercial and inquisitive, and as we can see, you are on your way to being that all once again.

Caravans

Caravans in ancient times were a form of mutual protection, like a convoy of ships in wartime. Travelling vast distances, across the Muslim lands and as ambassadors into the non-Muslim ones, caravans provided protection. The tent, so often used at the time of hajj, is still used by those living in the cities of the Middle East who often return to the desert to sleep under the stars, and without the use of sometimes alienating modern household appliances. Today and tomorrow, caravans of a sort will be seen - they will be for protection - Muslims will begin to and are moving around much more in so many communities. Where there is Islam to be taken, they are going. Remember, the best emigration is for Allah. Thus, those Muslims who were part of the Commonwealth emigrated to Britain where they have been for many generations, and if Allah wills, Muslims there are becoming a united and strong force. Those who saw the Big Lights, Bright City of the USA have gone there and are spreading Islam from New York to New Mexico, making it the fastest growing religion, as it is in Canada as well. So, Muslims emigrate to non-Muslim lands to seek knowledge, invite to Islam, and perform the intellectual and physical struggle in the way of Allah. However, the priority is in the aid of the Islamic world, so after your acquisition of knowledge, return to the Islamic world and impart that knowledge to your fellow Muslims.

Bridges

The bridge that helps you on your travels in seeking knowledge in the cause of Allah and the Muslims is the bridge that will grant you salvation, if Allah wills. Be it the Khwaju bridge at Isfahan or the Bridge over the Harba River, Samarra or the Golden Gate Bridge, San Francisco, make the journey for knowledge for Allah: 'We placed therein broad highways for them to pass through, that they may be guided.' (HQ, 18:107)

Hotels (*Khans*)

These are hostels where Muslims used to stay on their travels, such as the one found at Tash Kurgan, Afghanistan or the 'Great New Khan', Istanbul. Today, they would be hotels with modern conveniences such as the Burj Al-Arab, Dubai. Muslims must demand that the hotels they go to have halal food and it is prepared in a halal way - the purchasing power of a Muslim is going to increase because we will be the biggest market in Earth, if Allah wills, and therefore, asking hotels and hostels for services which are conducive to you, such as a prayer room and halal food, are what you are probably getting in some hotels, but will get in most, in the future.

Markets

Markets in the old Muslim world, which still exists today, had hierarchy and a system. This would include the bazaar, which was the commercial 'spine of the town, linking mosques, bathhouses, hotels and schools - a city in miniature, consisting of dozens of streets. These can be found in Aleppo, Syria and a modern day equivalent would be in Casablanca, Morocco which is the more commercial centre of the country. However, markets today are being turned into malls, superstores, super-retail centres and the like. A combination of Islam and the new mall is being done. The muezzin's calls the faithful to prayer via the sound system of the mall, when business comes to a halt, and the Muslims go to a mosque, built in every mall as is done in the United Arab Emirates - this is the way forward, and this scheme will be extending globally.

Bathhouses

Many people have heard of *hammams*, bathhouses, which used to fill the Islamic world, and were male only or female only. It was such a pleasure to go in to one after a hard day's work in the scorching sun, and take a bath and then chat with fellow Muslims. This was a sign of cleanliness. They still exist in Syria, Turkey, Jordan, and most of the Middle East. However, the future says that bathhouses of all Islamic types will be built around the world so that people can be clean and like to be clean once again. Cleanliness is inherent to Islam.

THE LANDSCAPE

Cities

'Between them and the cities which We had blessed,
We had placed cities in prominent positions, and We had made the stages of journey between them easy:
"Travel in them safely both by night and by day."' (HQ, 34:18)

If you are going to go into any city today, the buildings towards the centre are going to be much higher then they ever have been. This is because the most money can be found there, so rather than build wider, they take the natural approach and build upwards. Whereas as the sight of the Manhattan skyline made millions flock to America in search of prosperity, the skylines of all major Muslim cities are growing higher. With the concepts of Islam behind these building approaches, beautiful landscapes can be seen all around the world in Dubai and even the largest building in the world, the Petronas Towers of Malaysia, is in a Muslim country. We are on our way, if we put in the effort to become Muslims by conviction.

Towns, Villages, Jungles, Deserts, Tundras

As Islam penetrates the heart of the city and simultaneously all these areas, through the work of all Muslims, that is when Islamic architecture and infrastructure goes into its best stage - the richest diversity with One Message - that there is no god but Allah and Muhammad (pbuh) is His Messenger.

Islamic architecture and infrastructure is very important in the future as it will provide a system whereby if one part of the Islamic world is involved in a problem such as a natural disaster, the command will be heard and met as millions of Muslims help their fellow Muslims instantly because of the efficiency of the infrastructure. As there will be no bureaucracy because there will be one Islamic state with one Islamic policy on law and trade, one global Islamic ruler, one global Islamic government, and one Islamic World, life will be so much better.

THE SPHERE OF ART

**'Blessed is the Name of your Lord,
the Possessor of Majesty and Beauty.' (HQ, 55:78)**

Burckhardt states
'The substance of art is beauty; and this, in Islamic terms, is a divine quality and as such has a double aspect: in the world, it is appearance; it is the garb which, as it were, clothes beautiful beings and beautiful things; in God, however, or in itself, it is pure inward beauty; it is the divine quality which, among, all the divine qualities manifested in the world, most directly recalls pure Being.'

Islamic art is one of the finest manifestations of Islamic civilisations, Its most outstanding feature is the emphasis on calligraphy and decorative arts, Even today, calligraphy is the dominant art from. Quite naturally, it is verses from the Holy Qur'an that are used on religious as well as non-religious objects.

Art in the Islamic world showed the Islamic culture of each of the places where it was found. Under the Umayyads, Syria and Palestine had their own type of Islamic art which were different from the Islamic Art found in Central Asia under the Timurids. In the new Millennium, it is now possible to see the Islamic art of every type, from everywhere in the world.

Art in Islam should reflect the entire Spectrum of Islam - the Islamic culture embraces all styles, customs and traditions which are reflective of Islam and righteous Muslims. So Islamic Art and calligraphy on lanterns in China is equally at home as Islamic calligraphy and decoration inside the Blue Mosque in Istanbul.

Therefore let you creative juices flow energetically or in a relaxed manner, provided they are controlled in an Islamic way. Make sure that the art that is produced places Allah, Islam and Muslims as the most attractive and peoples in the world in all terms. It is testimony that even those with the very least knowledge about religion in the arts recognise and can admire the beauty and genius of Islamic Art.

Art of the Islamic world can be found in the beauty and versatile manuscripts of the Holy Qur'an, antiques, paintings, sculptures, miniatures, tiles, prayer mats, weapons, armour, bowls, doors - everything in this world has beauty written upon it. But only in the Islamic conception, is the beauty really found.

The use of the computer has a great impact on the beauty of Islam, as has the interaction between the Islamic world and others. For example, one of the best examples of Islamic art combining the sculpture of the modern world and the hadith of the Prophet (pbuh) are the 'Swords of Triumph' in Baghdad. More inshallah will be made around the globe, celebrating Allah.

The definition of Art makes it something which is creative. As long as your creativity is channeled in an Islamic manner, then art in the Millennium will only be Islamic.

All around the world, in our everyday lives, we will see the Beauty of Allah, in every living and non-living thing, which proves the fact there is no god but Allah.

**'Verily, all things We have created in proportion and measure.'
(HQ, 32:9)**

THE SPHERE OF ENTERTAINMENT & LEISURE

'Verily, those who believe and do righteous deeds, shall have Gardens of Firdaus for their entertainment wherein they dwell forever.'
(HQ, 18:107)

The Prophet (pbuh) said 'Many people waste two advantages - health and leisure.'

Entertainment and socialising primarily involves around the family - no single males or females should play a part unless they are children or they are in a group which includes their *mahram*, such as their brother and sister.

This free-mixing of the sexes is not fun unless you are married - imagine you arrive at an event with your wife/ husband, you separate and go into male/female-only areas. The men are socialising and talking about what men talk about and the ladies talk about what ladies like to talk about. The occasional glances of love between husband and wife from across the hall, and the acknowledgment that the night is still young, make marriage a sacred but fun institution.

Generalisations will only lead to complaints of stereotypes, but a lady must enjoy and celebrate her femininity and a man must celebrate his masculinity. Masculinity has certain attributes such as playing a very strenuous and dangerous sport such as rugby which ladies should not be playing. In a similar fashion, a man who likes to knit or sew in his social life as opposed to playing sport is missing out on the best that he can give his body and mind. Sometimes a lady needs to be with other ladies, a man with his friends, the married couple away from the children and the children away from the parents!

It is important that socialising and entertainment plays a part of the Muslim and that a balance is achieved. Entertainment and your leisure time should primarily be taken up by interacting with other people, majorly Muslims, of a variety of backgrounds and ages, visiting them, going out together for social occasions, and time must be taken out in the day for socialising. A balance must be achieved and these fine words must be remembered:

WHEN IT'S TIME TO WORK, WORK,
WHEN IT'S TIME TO PLAY, PLAY
WHEN IT'S TIME TO PRAY, PRAY

Special occasions of which there should be plenty in a Muslim's life also provide a backbone to your socialising. For children, their are youth clubs, which must be seen as hip, young, exclusive, happening places where health and sport must play a vital part. For adolescent males and females, they should be in youth clubs and settings which cater to their tastes. If they are not given these facilities, they become bored, and BOREDOM LEADS TO SEXUAL PROBLEMS AND CRIME. For married couples, there are a variety of functions and events they could attend as a couple, such as the cinema, going to a club, playing a sport, going to appropriate parties and celebrations.

Celebrate the Joy of Life

For the family as a whole the list is limitless and that is what Millennium Islam is about - making the family the centre of your life. Going to theme parks, circuses, museums, water parks, museums, restaurants, weddings, celebrations of births, university graduation and all events of goodness in a Muslim's life which will please Allah.

The Prayer on Friday is also a celebration of people as they gather in the mosque to pray in congregation and outside the mosque they chat about the past week's events:

'O you who believe!
When the call is proclaimed for the Friday Prayer, come to the remembrance of Allah and worship, and leave of business - that is better for you, if you but know! Then when the Friday Prayer is ended, you may disperse through the land, and seek the Bounty of Allah much: that you may be successful.'
(HQ, 62:9-10)

There are also days which are considered as a celebration for Muslims. These occasion are observed with devotion to seek the pleasure of Allah. There is no concept of festival only for pleasure. The festivals are the occasions of thanksgiving, joy and happiness. The two major occasions in Islam in each year are: Eid al-Fitr and Eid al-Adha.

Eid al-Fitr is observed at the end of the month of Ramadan. In Ramadan, a Muslim fasts from dawn to sunset, praying and seeking the pleasure of Allah, and after sunset they break the fast and CELEBRATE Allah's Bounty all around the world. There are celebrations for thirty whole nights thanking Allah that you survived the day and kept your fast in His Name. After a month of this fasting, Muslims express their happiness and love by offering a congregational prayer, and praising Allah for His Bounty. They express their gratitude to Allah for enabling them to observe fasting which is a very useful rigorous training programme. The day is generally observed as a holiday in Muslim countries and will be a holiday around the world in the future. Special dishes are prepared, international delicacies tasted, presents are given and received, people visit each other and have parties wearing their best clothes on this day.

Eid al-Adha begins on the 10th of Dhu'l Hijjah and continues until the 12th day of the month. It is celebrated to commemorate Prophet Ibrahim's (Abraham's) readiness to sacrifice his son Ismail (Ishmael) (may Allah be pleased with them) on the command of Allah. Allah accepted Ibrahim's devotion and obedience and asked him to sacrifice a lamb instead. The occasion of great importance comes every year during the Hajj (Pilgrimage to Mecca) and is observed by offering congregational prayer. After the prayer, the Muslims, who can afford it, sacrifice animals like goats, cows or camels, to seek Allah' s pleasure. The meat of the sacrificed animal is eaten and shared among the relatives, neighbours and the poor. The sacrifice expresses the inner feeling of a Muslim that, if need be, he will sacrifice his most loved possession for Allah. This is the lesson of the occasion. We must remember here that what Allah wants is not the animal nor its meat or blood, rather He wants our devotion and submission to His command.

Some other occasions to observe and celebrate include
Night of Power (Lailatul Qadr)
Night of Ascent (Lailat ul-Mi'raj)
The Beginning of Hajj (The Pilgrimage to Mecca)
The Dates of the Islamic Battles such as the Battle of Badr
The Birthday of the Prophet Muhammad (pbuh)

All aspects of entertainment and leisure, be it cinema, computer games, magazines, comics, sports, museums, celebrations and parties can be found in Islam. Everything, be it a magazine for teenagers or a serious film about relationships for adults, can be 'Islamised'.

The Straight Path is eternal and dynamic.

If an innovation in celebration comes,

it must mould its character into The Straight Path.

HALAL CINEMA AND TV - FILM WITH '*ILM* (Knowledge)

Cinema, television and all its offshoots, such as DVDs and IMAX, combine to create a very powerful medium - if executed well, you feel as if you are there. You feel you know the people on the screen, that they are standing straight in front of you. As everyone knows, power in the wrong hands is a very dangerous thing.

Cinema and television around the world has been abused more than it has been used for good. True, there is some excellent cinema and television out there sending the right messages and vibrations, but it is very limited in terms of all the garbage that is available and shown. Pornography of all decadent types, violence, mayhem, murder, all types of sin and sickness is more catered for than the good. This is because the market for these sin 'products' had been large - 'had been' - it will NOT BE NOW.

In Islam, cinema is designed for certain things such as

a) **About the Majesty of Allah**.
b) **About Prophet Muhammad** (pbuh) and his time such as 'The Message', whereby the Prophet (pbuh) was not depicted.
c) **About Islamic History** - all aspects, from science to children - every part of history.
d) **About Muslims around the world** - all aspects, from USA to the Sudan - around the whole globe.
e) **About the relations between the Muslim World and the non-Muslim world** such as 'The 13th Warrior' and 'Lawrence of Arabia'.

The qualities and style which would embody the Islamic Film and Television of the future would be the same that embodied Islam at the time of the Prophet Muhammad (pbuh). However, the content would be as varied as the wide spectrum of Islam. Intelligence, style, excite and grace would be part of these attributes.

For the children there would be exciting stories of Muslim heroes:
'With the launch of *Fatih, Sultan Muhammad*, Al-Fateh International Co, have ventured where every intelligent Muslim would like the Ummah to head to: a future which equates halal entertainment with excitement, imagination and real entertainment.' *Fatih* is the animated story of Mehmet II, the Ottoman Sultan also known as "the Conqueror" (an-Nasir) following his conquest of Constantinople in 857/1453

Comic book heroes such as Spider-man, Superman and Batman have shown a sense of the right morality - that good must win over evil. Children learn that to be the good guy is better than to be the bad guy, because you get the looks, the brains, the strength, the speed, the action, the fun, the excitement, you always win and you get the girl whom you'll get married to!

There would have to be a watershed, for programmes suitable for adults only, but which must still be on the Straight Path. No pornography or sick television and cinema would be tolerated - so the key must be that the imagination is stimulated more than the images. This is the rule for television for the Muslim adults who wish to discuss serious subjects:

THE LESS THAT IS SHOWN, THE GREATER THE IMPACT ON THE MIND

In some modern films, the imagination and mind are stimulated by what is not shown on the screen, but only indicated. For example, in a crime thriller, not showing the crimes can actually make the crimes committed in the film much more disturbing. When one is repulsed by what occurs in a crime thriller without actually seeing the graphic horrors committed, the message has more power.

Films from outside the world of Islam would be censored in an appropriate fashion and sick debauched behaviour would lead to the film being banned. There is a style from the non-Islamic world which if controlled such as that of cinema, as exhibited in some of the best films made, would be welcomed for it would show a culture which was more inclined towards the message of Islam than other cultures.

HALAL MUSIC

'And you will see the angels surrounding the Throne on all sides, singing Glory and Praise to their Lord. They will be judged with truth, and it will be said "Praise be to Allah, the Lord of the Worlds!"' (HQ, 39:75)

THE ECHOING MIXED SOUND OF A HUNDRED MUEZZINS CALLING THE FAITHFUL TO PRAYER ACROSS A CITY IS ONE OF THE MOST BEAUTIFUL TYPES OF MUSIC ON EARTH.

Some Muslims cannot understand why to some scholars music is banned in Islam, often referred to as 'idle talk'. It is largely because in the hadith which the Prophet Muhammad (pbuh) talked about with regards to the End of Time, say that 'singing and musical instruments will be widespread.' Some scholars have taken this to mean that this music is forbidden in Islam, a statement which though taken with the best of intentions, needs to be quantified.

Let us face reality. Most music today is about sex. The Prophet (pbuh) knew that this would happen, and that is why it is related in the hadith. Naturally, when a society starts to descend into moral decay, illicit sex, debauchery and decadence are key and obligatory policies and practices. Music, undoubtedly, would play a part in it, as it does. Visit any country, and music and singing is quite prevalent. The themes are what essentially matters.

A defocus on music and singing in Islam is needed.

WHEN THE CALL TO PRAYER IS HEARD, THE MUSIC STOPS

Music and singing about the Majesty of Allah.
This is by far the most legitimate and best excuse for music and singing. The Holy Qur'an when sung by a beautiful voice makes the skin shiver, with the love of Allah. Songs and Music can range from the Names of Allah, the bountiful actions of Allah for His people, His love for orphans - as long as the Majesty of Allah is the primary focus of the song, the list is endless. This is the music which should be prevalent in Muslim and non-Muslim countries.

Music and singing about Prophet Muhammad (pbuh).
In suitable praise for Muhammad (pbuh) and his actions as the Messenger of Allah, this is also another legitimate excuse for halal music. A balance must be achieved.

Music and singing about and for Muslims
This is legitimate if it is to raise the spirits of Muslims who strive in the way of Allah, in as varied circumstances as war, during manual labour in the fields or when held as a prisoner of war or in their daily lives. Also for Muslims who have pleased Allah with their tales of honour, bravery and good actions. A balance must be achieved.

Songs and music on righteous themes.
Songs which promote the good and forbid the evil and are valid.

Incidental Music
Music without any singing and which does not have hidden Satanic messages.

Music and singing about love in marriage, family life, and halal friendships
This is to be seen as a step towards Islam and away from the unlawful. The content of the song should be examined thorougly, and then it must be seen whether the music fits in the wide Spectrum of Islam.

THE CUTTING EDGE OF HALAL ENTERTAINMENT: ISLAM

THE SPHERE OF JIHAD

Jihad means to struggle in the Way of Allah -
the struggle has begun.

It includes every action from speaking out to presenting oneself on the battlefield solely for the sake of Allah.

Whether speaking or keeping silent, smiling or serious, joining a meeting or leaving it, every action taken to help the progress of humanity, whether by individual or communities, is included in the meaning of Jihad.

There are two types of Jihad, where the best defense is offense:

1) Defend yourself
- conquer your emotions, thoughts and actions
- through the Heart, and the Holy Qur'an

2) Defend Islam and Muslims
- through your Hands and your Tongues
- The intellectual attack - ORIENTALISM
- The physical attack - SURVIVAL & VICTORY

The only way to perform Jihad is to think, believe and practice the religion. Every objective, every action must be done in His Name, and for His Benefit, which it to help mankind.

'O believers!
If you help Allah,
Allah will help you and make your foothold firm.'
(HQ, 47:7)

ORIENTALISM - THE RESISTANCE AND THE VICTORY

As Professor Edward Said states, the reasons for Orientalism was essentially to 'manage - and even produce - the Orient (the Islamic world) politically, socially, militarily, ideologically, scientifically and imaginatively.' Orientalism has been described as 'ideological warfare' and a Muslim who tries to approach Orientalism is said to be in 'a bed of vipers'. In the present day, it has been stated that in Orientalism, the outright prejudices of non-Muslims such as Dante and Muir against Islam had now given way to a much more subtle approach.

Many of the same prejudices against Islam are said to remain, but are hidden beneath a cloak of apparent praise and sympathy but often in a form of subtle condescension. The ideological warfare of the non-Muslim upon the Muslim and the events described are still going on BUT WILL STOP. However, Orientalism as a force will no longer exist in the sphere of Millennium Islam, when Islam is the dominant force on this Earth.

The RESISTANCE IS ON. This is not a new phenomenon - it began centuries ago, whereby even the non-Muslim could see the truth from the falsehood, the light from the dark, the right from the wrong, as O'Leary states:

**'History makes it clear however,
that the legend of fanatical Muslims sweeping through the world and
forcing Islam at the point of the sword upon conquered races
is one of the most fantastically absurd myths that historians have ever repeated.'**

Professor Edward Said comments that Orientalism's university course taught at Oxford, Cambridge, Harvard and Tokyo, Oriental studies 'were to be thought not so much as scholarly activities but as instruments of national policy' against Muslim countries.

However, Orientalism today is dying as a force because proclaimed and affirmed Muslims are being accepted to study Orientalism (Islam from a Western view) at the best Western universities across the world. What the academia of these institutions want is that these intelligent Muslims, who not only believe with their heart about Islam but also their minds, act as a challenge for them and for their students.

Where there is a will, there's a way. Muslim students, professors and academics at these institutions who believe in Allah and the Last Day are manifestation of His Will. In the least likeliest of places, you find that Islam will emerge. Every country which wants to succeed on this Earth in material terms is advancing its Islamic Studies programme faster than any other subject. Islam is the future - a fact which the believer and non-believer, the intelligent and the simple, all know.

A MUSLIM WHO STUDIES ISLAM ANYWHERE IS PERFORMING JIHAD -
HE IS DEFENDING ISLAM INTELLECTUALLY

He tries to prove that there is no god but Allah, that the Holy Qur'an could not be written by the Prophet Muhammad for he could not read or write and other such academic studies of Islam. They try to prove Islam using clear evidence. But, who provides this information? It is Allah, who helps these Muslim students perform Jihad. He helps them in science, law, history, languages, art, architecture - every subject.

The guiding principle for Muslims who study Orientalism and also for those who study arts and sciences is one of the other names of the Holy Qur'an, 'al-Furqan' - Criterion, Distinction between Truth and Falsehood.

**'So obey not the disbelievers,
but strive against them by preaching with the utmost endeavour the Qur'an.'**
(HQ, 25:72)

**'O you who believe! If you obey and fear Allah,
He will grant you the Criterion to judge between Right and Wrong
or a Way to get out of every difficulty.'**
(HQ, 8:29)

THE THREAT WITHIN

However, the majority of Muslims who have studied Orientalism at these institutions in the present day are basically two types:

1) The present rulers and/or their sons and daughters of Muslim countries and rich Muslims' sons and daughters - largely all concerned are there for the experience at the University, and not the defense of Islam. They are Muslims, but their immense wealth and lifestyle makes them weak Muslims who regret their actions often. They want to be better Muslims.

2) 'Muslims' by name and not by nature - belonging to one of the 72 sects that will enter Hell. These sects, designed by criminals to subvert Islam, have wealth and power - they were entering the best educational institutions to deliberately subvert Islam, write thesis showing the lack of force of Islam in the future, helping criminals to form policies to hurt Muslims all around the world.

EXPECT THE UNEXPECTED

However, only Allah could come up with a plan whereby Orientalism becomes Islam. The Professors of Orientalism at these institutions did not count on the power of Allah to make two very important events occur:

1) The minute number of Muslims students, professors and academics who are let in to defend Islam, and it is seen as to how they can be broken, like how a lion can be tamed, like a wild stallion broken. The taming is essentially to make them not really believe in Islam in their minds. However, what happens when every argument that is placed before the student is invalid in the light of his knowledge of Islam? What if every time he is asked Orientalist questions, he can counter-argue each one effectively with Islamic answers? What if he has fully comprehended the power of the first Divine words to the Prophet Muhammad (pbuh): "Read! Read in the name of your Lord, Allah Who has created" (HQ, 96:1) and every problem that is thrown at him is answered with the knowledge of Islam? This is the time when Allah has turned the tide.

2) What if the non-Muslim students, professors and academics today studying Islam can longer face the simple fact that Islam is the Truth? They will convert and they are converting to Islam. Decades ago, these same Professors would have expelled the Orientalist students because they were training them to become spies like Lawrence of Arabia, civil servants, diplomats and businessmen, so if they became Muslims, they would be classified as 'traitors', for the sake of national security. Today, it is accepted sombrely as a fact that these non-Muslims who were being groomed to help their countries, have gone 'native' and believe in that 'ancient' religion of Islam.

'Verily, this is the Word that separates the Truth from Falsehood.' (HQ, 86:13)

There are those non-Muslims who do not convert, but they understand the religion and its beauty better than those Muslims who are only Muslim by name. They sympathise with the plight of these people and they marvel at the achievements of their Prophet (pbuh), and how that seventh-century old preaching is the dynamic force of the new Millennium. It is indeed Praiseworthy of Allah, when these non-Muslims studying Islam and learn Arabic, use words such as Asalaamualaikum, Bismillah, Inshallah and Alhamdililah which will become part of the English language.

Gone are the days when Dante in Inferno described Muhammad (pbuh) as being in Hell, for saying that Jesus was not God. The attitudes of Orientalists have now changed. The taint of the word Orientalism and the imagery associated with that word now means that attitudes are forced to change, with the authors now calling themselves Islamicists; an interesting choice of word considering that those who Muslims who wish to Islamise their way of life in every way possible, but primarily politically, are called Islamists.

Additionally, Orientalism has been a major factor in bring a major change in the way Islam is perceived at the beginning of the twentieth century. Men like Lawrence of Arabia, an Oxford-educated Arabist, acting in the name of British imperialism, have given way to a European academic elite who discuss Islam and many of whom embrace it wholeheartedly.

THE ISLAMICIST = THE ISLAMIST?

The tide has changed. The Cambridge Illustrated History of The Islamic World, 1999 dedication reads 'To my Muslim friends.' This is their defense of modern present-day scholarship in the field of Islam and it certainly demands considerable merit:

> 'Those involved in this tradition of scholarship considered themselves committed to the objective study of the Islamic world. In recent years, however, and in particular since the publication of Edward Said's *Orientalism* in 1978, these scholars have been accused of distorting truth, that is of practicing 'orientalism.' The charges are that they have explained Islam in terms of some unchanging essence rather than subject to processes of differentiation and change similar to those undergone by the West, that they have created a body of received truths about Islam which have authority in western academic life but little relation to Muslim realities, that they have in fact **created a structure of knowledge to explain superiority of the West over the Islamic world, and to justify its continuing domination. There is a grain of truth in these charges, and more than a grain when we come to the popular discourse of politicians and the press. But these charges are less fairly applied to the twentieth-century masters of Islamic studies. And they are less fairly applied to most practitioners of the subject in recent decades, who bring the insights of all disciplines from anthropology to psychology to their research, who more often than not work side by side with Muslims in their studies, and who reveal the many different ways there have been and are of being Muslim.**'

They are our friends, but there is still a distance which Allah will bridge, if He wills:

> 'The only major literacy Islamic source before 800 is the Qur'an, which **modern Islamicists generally regard as a collection of Muhammad's own utterances.**'

However, they are not Muslims yet, but, if Allah wills, the Islamicist will become the Islamist - a real Muslim.

THE SIMPLETON & THE PHILOSOPHER

In most of the best universities of the world, the most simple of religions, where the concept of One God called Allah is preached universally, is given the most attention with regards to discussion and dialogue. Islam is one of the most intellectual subjects currently being discussed around the world, be it at Harvard, Oxford or Cambridge University or The Centre for Islamic Studies, Tokyo. It is ironic that 'One God, One God', the words spoken by Bilal (may Allah be pleased with him), the Muslim Abyssinian slave, as his owner, Umayya placed huge rocks upon his chest, is seen as the most intellectual concept on Earth and such a 'hot' media topic. And why not - the irony is that the most simple and the most intellectual thoughts are those concerning Allah.

There are those Muslims who should go well-prepared to these universities to study the West's view of Islam and to bridge this gap. Challenge theories and concepts about Islam, correct the incorrect ones, embrace the valid ones, and guide your colleagues and teachers towards a better understanding of the religion. Your Guide is Allah and the Muslims who surround you and whom you trust.

The Prophet (pbuh) said
'Whoever travels on a path seeking in it knowledge,
Allah will smooth for him a path leading by it to the Garden.'

'He it is Who has sent His Messenger with Guidance and the Religion of Truth
to make it victorious over all other religion, even though the disbelievers hate it.'
(HQ, 61:9)

JIHAD

THE PHYSICAL DEFENSE: SURVIVAL AND VICTORY

Around the world, the twentieth century has seen many wars fought against Muslims or instigated between Muslims. Reading the Holy Qur'an will show that these themes are not new, and will appear in the Millennium.

The Independent : **'In recent years Muslims have been the greatest sufferers from state terrorism'**

'Those who believe, and suffer exile with might and main in Allah's Cause, with their goods and their lives, they have the highest rank in the sight of Allah.' (HQ, 9:20)

'Permission to fight is given to those believers who are fighting them, because they have been wronged, and surely, Allah is Able to give them Victory.' (HQ, 22:29)

'Those who have been expelled from their homes unjustly only because they said: "Our Lord is Allah."' (HQ, 22:40)

THE PERSECUTION HAS TO STOP

All around the world, be it in Asia, Europe or Africa - Muslims were being wiped out for being Muslims. When Muslims cried for help, only a few Muslims came - it was non-Muslims who helped to stop the persecution, because they had their own agenda. The time has come for Muslims to unite in defense against oppression, persecution, murder, rape, and all the other atrocities that are being committed on them. No more Muslims will suffer if we unite our forces. If you are in the north, the south will help, if you are in the east, the west will help - it will all be Muslims helping each other.

Torture weapons and security equipment is what many governments in Muslim countries use to suppress Muslims from practicing their faith. As the faith is rising, so is the method and intensity of the torture. Technology is being used for some of the most horrific and sickening types of torture by these governments on their citizens. Today, advances in technology have made it possible for military regimes to survive for a while in the face of massive popular discontent. It is believed that if you spend enough money, you can defeat even the most ingenious infiltrators or the most popular revolt. However, it is The Truth which makes man survive, and us all Muslims will have to be patient and strive in the Cause of Allah - He is sending His Force from amongst YOU.

Christians, Jews, Hindus, Buddhists, Sikhs and also those who believe in a religion with the concept of the Creator, were born all born Muslims, but they were raised those religions. All those religions contain grains of truth, but it is only Islam which is the Complete Truth and nothing but The Truth.
However, we must remain vigilant and vigilance always pays.

The Hypocrites

The Prophet (pbuh) said these are each the sign of a hypocrite: 'When he speaks, he lies. Whenever he promises, he always breaks it. If you trust him, he proves to be dishonest. Whenever he quarrels, he behaves in very impudent, evil, insulting manner. Whenever he makes a covenant, he proves himself treacherous.'

We must guard against those who are working against us, as hypocrites within our Ummah and outside with our enemies who may come from any group, be it the atheists or the Christians, Jews, Hindus, Sikhs, Buddhists, Zoroastrians - whomever and wherever the criminals are, we will fight them.

'They plot and plan, and Allah plans, and Allah is the Best of Planners.' (HQ, 8:30)

However, we must be patient and also realise that the enemies of today can be the fellow Muslims of tomorrow, and it is our righteous conduct which will make them that, by the Grace of Allah. Israel is just one - around the world Muslims are being persecuted, murdered, raped, tortured - in Africa, Asia, America, Europe, everywhere:

IT HAS TO STOP - Muslims must defend their own people and you will.
Allah has made the Muslims the strongest and bravest entity on Earth if they obey Him Alone.

JIHAD=PARADISE

THE BEST COMMERCE

'O you who believe! Shall I guide you to a commerce that will save you from an a painful torment? That you believe in Allah and His Messenger and that you strive hard in the Cause of Allah with your wealth and your lives; that will be better for you, if you but know! He will forgive you your sins, and admit you into the Gardens under which rivers flow and pleasant dwellings in 'Adn Paradise; that is the great success.' (HQ, 6:10-11)

THE PROMISE OF ALLAH

'Verily, Allah has purchased of the believers their lives and their properties;
for the price that theirs shall be the Paradise.
They fight in Allah's Cause, so they kill others and are killed.
It is a promise in Truth, which is binding on Him in the Torah and the Gospel and the Qur'an.
And who is truer to His Covenant than Allah? Then rejoice in the bargain which you have concluded.
That is the supreme success!' (HQ, 9:111)

THE PLEDGE OF ALLEGIANCE TO THE BEST MUSLIM AMONGST YOU

'Verily , those who give the Pledge of Allegiance to you (O Muhammad),
they are in fact giving the Pledge to Allah.' (HQ, 48:10)

WHOMEVER YOU ARE, JIHAD IS YOUR KEY TO PARADISE

'March forth whether you are light (being healthy, young and wealthy) or heavy (being ill, old and poor)
and strive hard with your wealth and your lives in the Cause of Allah.
This is better for you if you but knew.'
(HQ, 9:41)

'If you march not forth, He will punish you with a painful torment and will replace you with another people and you cannot harm Him at all, and Allah is Able to do all things' (HQ, 9:39)

'O you who believe! What is the matter with you,
that when you are asked to march forth in the Cause of Allah, you cling heavily to the Earth?
Are you pleased with the life of this world rather than the Hereafter?
But little is the enjoyment of this world compared to the Hereafter.'(HQ, 9:38)

THE REWARD

'Jihad is ordained for you though you dislike it, and it may be that you dislike a thing which is good for you and that you like a thing which is bad for you. Allah knows but you do not know.' (HQ, 2:216)

COMPETE TO BE THE BEST

'Not equal are those of the believers who sit at home except those who are disabled
and those who strive in the Cause of Allah with their wealth and their lives.
Allah has preferred in grades those who strive hard and fight with their wealth and their lives
above those who sit at home. Unto each Allah has promised Paradise,
but Allah has preferred those who strive hard and fight, above those who sit by a huge reward.' (HQ, 4:95)

'O you who believe! Fight the disbelievers who are close to you, and let the find firmness in you:
and know that Allah is with those who fear Him.'
(HQ, 9:123)

IT IS ALLAH WHO WILL HELP YOU, SO REMEMBER HIM

'O you who believe!
When you meet an enemy force take a firm stand against them and
remember the Name of Allah much, so that you may be successful.' (HQ, 8:45)

THE UNITED

'And consult them in the affairs.' (HQ, 3:159)

'And who conduct their affairs by mutual consultation.' (HQ, 42:38)

FIGHT IN THE CAUSE OF ALLAH

'Those who believe fight in the Cause of Allah,
and those who disbelieve, fight in the cause of Satan.
So go and fight against the friends of Satan: ever feeble is the plot of Satan.'
(HQ, 4:176)

THE BRAVE

'O you who believe! When you meet those who disbelieve in a battlefield, never turn your backs to them.'
(HQ, 8:15)

THE CHASE IS ON

'So do not become weak against your enemy, nor be sad,
and you will be superior in victory if you are indeed true believers.'
(HQ, 3:319)

'And don't be weak in the pursuit of the enemy.
If you are suffering hardships, they are suffering similar hardships,
but you have hope from Allah while they have none. Allah is All-Knowing, All-Wise.' (HQ, 4:104)

HONOURING THE RELIGION WITH YOUR ACTIONS

The Prophet (pbuh) said
'Proceed in the Name of Allah and for Allah, and upon the religion of Allah's Messenger.
Do not kill the very old or a child or a woman and do not go to extremes and exceed the limits.
Collect the war booty, reconcile, and do good as Allah loved those who do good.'

THE VICTORY OF ALLAH

Ali ibn Abi Talib said to Umar ibn Khattab (may Allah be pleased with them):
'O Chief of the believers! This matter cannot be 'victory or defeat' because of a great number or because of a small number but it is His religion which He has made superior and His troops which He has honoured and supported with angels till it reached as far as it has reached. We have been promised victory by Allah, and Allah fulfils His Promise and supports His troops.'

BE PREPARED: THE HELP OF ALLAH IS NEAR

'Do you think that you enter Paradise without such trails as came to those who passed away before you?
They were afflicted with severe poverty and ailments and were so shaken that even the Messenger and those who believed along with him said,
"When will the Help of Allah come?" Yes! Certainly, the Help of Allah is near!' (HQ, 2:214)

THE UNSEEN - HELP SENT UNDER THE COMMAND OF ALLAH

The power of the Unseen is what makes Islamic Defensive Strategy the best there ever has been or ever will be. We are not cowards and can never run from a war when we or another community is being oppressed and persecuted. We know that whatever power the aggressor may have, whether they have nuclear force machine guns or spears, we know that nothing can stop us, provided Allah is with us. When Allah is with us, no army, no law, no war on this Earth can stop us.

The Prophet (pbuh) believed in the Unseen, as any Muslim could. He did not know the Unseen, for only Allah knows the Unseen: **'Say: "I do not tell to you that I have the treasures of Allah in my possession, nor do I know the Unseen, nor do I say to you that I am an angel. I only follow what has been revealed to me."'** (HQ, 6:50).

The Holy Qur'an describes how Muslims managed to emerge victorious on the Day of Hunayn even though they had just been so close to the jaws of defeat:

> 'Allah has given you victory on many battlefields, including the Day of Hunayn, when your great numbers delighted you but did not avail you in any way; and the Earth seemed narrow to you all for all its great breadth; then you turned back in flight. **Then Allah sent down His Reassurance on His Messenger and on the believers, and sent down troops you did not see, and punished the disbelievers.** That is the recompense of the disbelievers.' (HQ, 9:25-26)

So the feeling of tranquillity which enabled the Prophet (pbuh) and the believers to stand firm without anxiety was Allah's Help, for he sent invisible soldiers. Who were these invisible soldiers? A power emanating from the Unseen. Today few minds are capable of comprehending that great battle's sudden turnabout was due to a mysterious and invisible aid from the Unseen, under direct command from Allah, the Almighty.

THE BATTLE OF BADR

The Battle of Badr was 'The Day of Criterion' (HQ, 8:41)

THE PAGANS

Commanded by Abu Sufyan, the Meccan army consisted of 1,100 fighters including 600 soldiers in armour and 200 cavalry. They worshipped idols of stone and rock. Before they left for the battle, a thousand warriors gathered in the shrine of idols, and a hundred horseman lined outside, where they placed their arms near the foot of the temple. Lifting their arms in supplication, the Quraysh looked at the god of War which resided in the idol of Hobol. To him they sang hymns and sought a sign for victory of against the Prophet of Allah (pbuh); but no sign came. When they left for the battle, they were accompanied by singers and dancers. Whenever the army halted, dancing and drinking parties were held. The soldiers' shining armours, set and determined faces and gleaming swords were a pageant of colour, as were the groups of dancing girls, who, with sparkling eyes, radiant faces, dressed in their gala dresses, thumping on their tambourines, came dancing along the line of the soldiers. The army was arrogant, and boasted of its invincibility because of its military power and numerical strength. They were only fighting to prove their superiority over the Muslims, not because of any ideal or ideology.

THE MUSLIMS

Commanded by The Prophet (pbuh), the Muslim army was made up of 313 fighters. Of these, 86 were Emigrants from Mecca and the rest were the Helpers of Medina. Such was the scarcity of resources that only two or three Muslims had horses. The force were small in number, weak in defense, ill-fed, and ill-equipped and loving no idol - the Quraysh thought they would emerge victorious. The number of camels was no more than 70 so that three or four persons took turns on each camel. The Prophet (pbuh) took turns to ride the camel with two people. When they asked him to ride the camel to exclude themselves from the turns, the Prophet (pbuh) answered:

'You are no better in strength than me. Concerning the reward, I am not in less need of it than you.'

At the battlefield, Prophet Muhammad (pbuh) raised his hands high in supplication:

'O Allah! Quraysh has come with all its arrogance, trying to brand Your Prophet a liar.
O Allah! Help me against them as You promised,

because if our small group perishes today nobody will remain to worship You.'

At the battle, sabres and scimitars rose and fell; lances and spears and arrows were doing their evil, the shouting and yelling of warriors blending with the thud-thudding of women's drums, their cymbals clashed, war chants rented the air, roars and battle cries mingled, again and when the Quraysh charged to dislodge the Muslims, each time they were repulsed. The Muslims rose, to see legions of Quraysh retreating, as quick as their legs could carry them. Leaving their dead on the field, they fled.

It is difficult to conceive of so small a group prevailing over such a great army with all its arms and armour unless one believes in the Direct Intervention and Support of Allah. Some of the mysteries of that battle were revealed in the following verses of the Holy Qur'an:

'Allah has already made you victorious at Badr when you were weak, so fear Allah, in order that perhaps you may be grateful. When you (O Muhammad) said to the believers, "Is it not enough for you that you Lord assisted you with **three thousand angels**, sent down? Yes, indeed! If you are steadfast and fear Allah and the time they come upon you suddenly, your Lord will assist you with **five thousand angels**, clearly identified. Allah only did this as good news for you and as an assurance to your hearts. There is no victory except from Allah, the Almighty, the All-Wise.'
(HQ, 3:123-126)

'When your Lord revealed to the angels,
"Verily, I am with you, so make those who believe firm.
I will cast terror into the hearts of those who disbelieved,
so strike their necks and strike all their finger joints!"'
(HQ, 8:12)

'You did not kill them - it was Allah who killed them:
and you did not throw, when you threw - it was Allah who threw.'
(HQ, 8:17)

These are some aspects of the Unseen secrets and the Support of Allah which came to the assistance of this small group, weak in terms of number but strong in terms of morale, in order to implement everlasting justice by means that could be neither seen nor heard.

'Verily, We have given you a manifest victory that Allah may forgive you (O Muhammad)
your sins of the past and the future and complete His Favour upon you,
and guide you on the Straight Path,
and that Allah may help you with strong help.'
(HQ, 48:1-4)

Allah will send these forces to help the Muslims again, till they have the victory.
But the Muslims MUST KNOW THEIR OWN STRENGTH WHICH IS FROM THE LOVE OF ALLAH:

'O Prophet! Urge the believers to fight.
If there are 20 STEADFAST BELIEVERS, THEY WILL OVERCOME 200,
and if there are 100, THEY WILL OVERCOME 1000 DISBELIEVERS,
because they are people who do not understand.

Now Allah has lightened your task for He knows there is weakness in you.
So if there are **20 BELIEVERS, THEY SHALL OVERCOME 200,**
and if there are 1000 OF YOU, THEY SHALL OVERCOME 2000,
BY THE WILL OF ALLAH.
AND ALLAH IS WITH THE PATIENT.'
(HQ, 8:65-66)

YOU HAVE THE POWER TO BE THE BEST -
ATTAIN THE VICTORY OF HIS RELIGION.

JIHAD - THE JOINT ISLAMIC HUMANITY ALLIANCE for DEFENSE

An Islamic Defense Alliance will be set up, such as the Joint Islamic Humanity Alliance for Defense (JIHAD). This will seek to combat acts of foreign aggression, possible disputes within the Islamic world and also as an Human Intervention Body for those non-Muslims in areas of conflict who request the humanitarian aid of the Islamic State and have been confirmed as a community in the Islamic State.

THE JIHAD COUNCIL

This body will be formed by creating a Military Councillor from each Muslim state. They shall appoint a Secretary General for JIHAD. The JIHAD Council will be responsible for all executive and policy decisions. Only a decision which is taken by absolute consensus will be followed. The General Headquarters of JIHAD will be based in Arabia - with a view to uniting the voices of Islam.

THE DEFENSE ADVISORY COUNCIL

This body will be formed by creating a Military Advisory Council with a Councillor from each Muslim state within the Islamic world. The Defense Advisory Council will monitor the security needs of Muslim states, internal and external security and security needs of the region, financial regulation and administration for JIHAD.

THE MILITARY COUNCIL

This body will be formed by creating a Military Council with a Military Commander from each Muslim state within the Islamic world. It will come under direct supervision of the JIHAD Council. The Head of Armed Forces for each member state will be act as a representative for their own region. The head of the organisation, elected by all heads of state armed forces, will be known as the Allied Chief of Staff of JIHAD. The Military Council liaise with the JIHAD Council to form one decision and have one Islamic policy and the Military Council will execute the commands.

THE ISLAMIC MILITARY COMMANDS

Each Muslim state will come under a Military Command depending on their geographical location.

'O you who believe! Endure and be more patient than your enemy, and guard your territory by stationing army units permanently at the places from where the enemy can attack you, and fear Allah, so that you may be successful.' (HQ, 3:200)

THE ISLAMIC RAPID DEPLOYMENT FORCE

A rapid deployment force comprising at least 200,000 trained armed personnel fully equipped with the means of modern warfare with a complete range of air, sea, land and space military equipment shall be used to meet the external and internal threat to the security of the Islamic world. This force shall be capable of swift mobilisation in reaching all areas to meet all challenges in the case of emergencies.

'Verily, Allah loves those who fight in His Cause in rows as if they were a solid structure.'
(HQ, 61:4)

'And also He will give you another blessing which you love
and help from Allah and a near victory. And give glad tidings to the believers.' (HQ, 62:13)

There are three sanctuaries on this Earth:
1) The Ka'aba at Mecca where pilgrimage takes place
2) The Holy Prophet's Mosque, Medina
3) Al-Aqsa Mosque, Jerusalem where the Night Ascension to the Heavens took place -
MUSLIMS MUST HAVE ACCESS TO ALL - UNLIMITED ACCESS

THE MUSLIMS MUST UNITE,
GIVE ALLEGIANCE TO THE BEST AMONGST THEM, AND PERFORM JIHAD -
ESTABLISH ALLAH'S KINGDOM ON THE EARTH

THE SPHERE OF THE MODEL

Do not presume the title is referring to modelling on a catwalk or in fashion magazines. Rather, this is the True Model - all Muslims have the Perfect Muslim to try to emulate, Muhammad (pbuh).

'Indeed in the Messenger of Allah you have a good example to follow for him who hopes for the Meeting with Allah and the Last Day, and remember Allah much.' (HQ, 32:21)

He was the Best of Mankind, and was fully human, flesh and bone, like you and me. He embodied the highest virtues of mankind and he has left his Sunnah to us, his way of life as recorded in authentic hadiths. As we know how he lived his life, from the way he conducted his marital life to the way he prayed, then we can try to emulate and acquire some of his attributes. Therefore, he is our first stop on how to be a Muslim.

Some groups in this community are doing the Prophet (pbuh) a disservice when they believe their actions, words and thoughts reflect those of the Prophet (pbuh) but they don't. They think they are emulating him by adorning a turban and dressing in the Arabic *thob* and are becoming more concerned with the ritual of Islam. For example, because Muhammad (pbuh) used a miswak to clean his teeth, Muslims in some modern countries are throwing away toothbrushes and electric toothbrushes some of which do wonders for the teeth, just because the Prophet (pbuh) used a miswak. An extension of these unIslamic rituals, mean that we should all go and live EXACTLY like the Prophet (pbuh) did, in the desert in seventh-century Arabia. GET REAL! The Holy Qur'an addresses itself to 'those who think', so think. The miswak emphasises that you must brush and clean your teeth, and because it has religious significance, it must be used with a toothbrush or an electric toothbrush, for the teeth will then become much more CLEANER. YOU MUST THINK - apply this example to all those rituals which are habits of the Prophet (pbuh), where the essence of the habit such as brushing teeth is kept, but the habitual action of seventh-century Arabia does not have to be emulated. The Holy Qur'an is addressed to 'those who think', 'those who listen', 'those who understand' - do not forget to THINK!

It is important that all Muslims to recognise that the Way of the Prophet (pbuh) has an essence, which is contained in his virtues and actions. There is the essence of his manners, the essence of his clothes, the essence of his administration as opposed to the actual incidents. Do not try to re-live the life of the Prophet (pbuh) step by step - look at his Way, and apply its essence. Copying him to the point of absurdity, makes these actions unIslamic, for they go to the extremes, and mock the religion of Islam rather than promote it. There are those who renounce this world and try to re-create seventh century Arabia. This action is unIslamic. Allah has asked us to ask for goodness in this world and in the Hereafter, with entry to the Paradise of Firdaus being the main aim of life. Living like a hermit or condemning others who wish to live in this world will not get you to Firdaus - establishing Islam and the Kingdom of Allah will. Thus, the Way of the Prophet (pbuh) is clear:

THE WAY OF THE PROPHET (pbuh)

RELIGIOUS WORSHIP OF ALLAH - must be performed as the Prophet (pbuh) advised.

VIRTUOUS ISLAMIC THOUGHTS, WORDS AND ACTIONS - must be followed as the Prophet (pbuh) advised.

ISLAMIC LEGISLATION - WHAT IS PERMITTED AND WHAT IS FORBIDDEN - must be followed as the Prophet (pbuh) advised and prescribed.

HABITUAL ACTIONS OF THE PROPHET (PBUH) - The Essence of the Habit can be followed such as cleaning teeth as prescribed, but adopting the habit in the vein of seventh-century Arabia is WRONG.

FOLLOW THE ESSENCE: ENJOIN THE GOOD, FORBID THE EVIL

Muhammad (pbuh) is, was and always will be THE BEST. However, he is not a god and though many rightly talk about his good deeds and his character, they essentially forget something:
HIS POWERFUL UNIQUE PERSONALITY

Muslims believe Muhammad (pbuh) was an amazingly virtuous person who only did good deeds - this is true - however, by comparing him to the stereotype you have of a holy man today limits him entirely, and it is this that his Sunnah reveals. If one Muslim was to read his Sunnah and about his life as a whole rather than just the parts used by Imams today for their speeches, one soon realises the true beauty of Islam. No other religion on Earth exists whereby religious documents such as hadith contain wit, humour as well as a code on how to live life. Whilst in the real world, the dynamism has gone and the old man with the white beard is regarded as holy just because he looks like (what some to perceive to be) the part, a Muslim in the Millennium when he reads some of the hadith which are part of the Path of Islam will realise the true character of Muhammad (pbuh), the man - how he coped with domestic events in the home to how he organised military campaigns against the Roman and Persian Empires. For this riveting material, read on.

He was the Prophet (pbuh). He was a man, but he was a unique man, the best man. To show this very clearly and in very simple, Allah Almighty instructed Prophet Muhammad (pbuh):

'Say: "I am only a human being like yourselves. It is revealed to me."' (HQ, 18:110)

There some groups from amongst this Muslim nation have exaggerated ideas about the Prophet (pbuh), who though he was the Best of Mankind, was fully human, flesh and bone, a descendant of Adam (may Allah be pleased with him):

The Prophet (pbuh) said: 'Do not exaggerate in praising me as the Christians praised Isa, the son of Maryam, for I am only a slave. So call me the slave of Allah and His Messenger.'

You must rid yourselves of some of the reprehensible innovations that have influenced your perception of Muhammad (pbuh), and remember that even the other people chosen for missions by Allah, like Jesus and Moses, still acknowledge and believe that Muhammad was the best. He said to Abu Bakr about his education 'Allah has given me the best of training.' When Prophet Jesus (may the peace of Allah be upon him) comes in the near future to contend with the False Messiah, he will state that he is a Muslim, that there is no God but Allah and that Muhammad is His Messenger. It is only Muhammad (pbuh) who occupies this position, and that is why his Sunnah is so clear for those that Allah makes it clear for.

Muhammad (pbuh) and His Holy Qur'an was the Best Miracle that Allah ever created for mankind - he was the best in every field. He had achieved a pinnacle of every good quality and his manners, character and career were a miracle in themselves.

There is a man who is a specialist - he specialises in one field and excels.
There is he who is a jack of all trades - he is competent but does not excel at all fields.
There is a jack of all trades, and a master of some -
rare, but it does happen that the specialist specialises in a variety of fields.
Then, there is Muhammad (pbuh)- the specialist and master in every field.
If you achieve perfection in a single quality to the extent that you surpass your peers, this is called genius.
If you achieve the peak in oratory, you are called a genius.
If you excel in the art of language, you are called a genius.
If you reach the apex of leadership, your are called a genius.
If you have a superb grasp of the art of war, you are called a genius.
If you are the finest legislator, you are a genius.

But a man who possesses all these talents and when he is put to the test attains the summit in each without having gone to school or having a teacher, such a man can only be a miracle.
And the only explanation for this, if it happens, is that such a man must be a prophet who is supported and helped by Allah the Generous. That man was, is and will always be Muhammad (pbuh).

Prophet Muhammad (pbuh) said
'Knowledge is my capital. Good sense is the basis of my religion. Love is my creed.
Longing for Allah is my carriage. Remembrance of Allah is my friend. Sorrow is my companion.
Patience is my dress. Truthfulness is my justification. Knowledge is my weapon.
Jihad is my morality. Prayer is my joy.'

Physical Description of the Prophet (pbuh)

By all accounts, he was exceptionally handsome. He was of average height. He had a large head, very black thick hair, a broad, noble forehead, very wide pensive and glittering eyes with dark black pupils and long eyelashes, a thick beard, a broad, muscular, chest and shoulders, and broad palms and feet. He had a fine, noble, straight and slightly aquiline nose, set proportionately over a large mouth in a lean face, a gap between his teeth, a long handsome neck, and his large, arched eyebrows were joined by light hairs. His skin was light coloured, of brown-sallow complexion. His face was filled with blessed radiance and brightness, and was often compared to a moon. He was well-built without being fat, and his body was firm and muscular, giving the impression of conspicuous strength with youthful energy and vitality. He used to walk with firm steps, bending forward with his eyes lowered to the ground. When he walked, it was as if descending a hill - none could be faster. His Companions (may Allah be pleased with them) found it difficult to keep pace with him. Though fast, his steps were sharp and firm. His figure tilted slightly forward as he moved around, as if was on a definite errand. His appearance had the mark of deep thought and contemplation.

However, it was his eyes which more than anything else seemed to convey some of his great spiritual and psychological strength and some of his iron resolve and singleness of mind, his total reliance on Allah. They beamed with his characteristic serenity and firm determination, giving the feeling of the authority of a commander. In general, they reflected the vast reservoir of intelligence and discernment, and contributed much to his awe-inspiring appearance.

Character of the Prophet (pbuh)

It is good to show the many sides of a man's personality, and his attributes.

REFLECTIONS

He had a reflective and thoughtful trait in his character. He was often deep in thought, often silent and only spoke when it was important to do so.

A MAN WITH A SENSE OF HUMOUR

He was more inclined to smile than laugh, however sometimes when he laughed, one could see his molars (back teeth). He was happy and content and had a good sense of humour, and would share his jokes. He never became angry on account of any personal slight.

THE MAN OF ISLAM

He did not avenge himself on anybody, only becoming angry for the sake of truth and Islam. But when that happened nothing could withstand his anger. He never struck anybody except for Allah's sake. He freely forgave and brushed aside personal insults. However, he showed great anger when a matter of principle was mocked or violated. But personal indignities and little insults would not make him angry, nor would they make him retaliate against his offenders.

THE MAN OF THE HOUSE

He was also industrious, never found just doing nothing. Even at home, he would take part in the household work of his wives. When there was nothing to be done, he would deem it his duty to amuse them, making them laugh with happiness. He quite often attended to his personal chores, washing and sewing his clothes, and mending his shoes, etc. He would not speak without a need or a purpose. He was given to the loaded expressive sentence, not too long, not too short, but sufficient. His manners were fine, neither coarse nor unfriendly nor meek or insignificant. He was never angry for personal motives.

THE PROBLEM ELIMINATER

He would say things which would make people overcome their vices and weaknesses.

THE MAN WHOM THE CHILDREN PLAYED WITH

Often, when he was not busy in some serious matter, a little girl from the neighbourhood would dash into his house, take him by the hand and demand 'Let us go out and play.' He would obey her and she would spin him about playing merry-go-round.

'Out of all that rubbish of Arab idolatries, argumentative theologies, traditions, subtleties, rumours and hypotheses of Greeks and Jews, with their idle wire-drawings, this wild man of the desert, with his wild sincere heart, earnest as death and life, with his great flashing natural eyesight, had seen into the kernel of the matter. idolatry is nothing:

"These wooden idols of yours, ye rub them with oil and wax, and the flies stick on them - these are wood, I tell you! They can do nothing for you; they are an impotent blasphemous pretence: a horror and abomination, if ye keep them. God alone has power: He made us, He can kill us and keep us alive; 'Allah akbar',
God is Great. Understand that His Will is the best for you; that however sore to flesh and blood,
you will find it the wisest, best; you are bound to take it so;
in this world and in the next, you have no other thing that you can do!"

And now, if the wild idolatrous men did believe this, and with their fiery hears laid hold to it, in what form soever it came to them, I say it is well worthy of being believed.'

Thomas Carlyle
"Heroes and Hero-worship"

'If GREATNESS OF PURPOSE, SMALLNESS OF MEANS AND ASTOUNDING OF RESULTS
are the three criteria of human genius, who could dare to compare any great men in history with Muhammad?

The most famous men created arms, laws and empires only. They founded, if anything at all, no more than material powers which often crumbled away before their eyes. This man Muhammad moved not only armies, legislation, empires, peoples and dynasties, but millions of men; and more than that the altars, the gods, the religions, the ideas, the beliefs and the souls.

On the basis of a Book, every letter of which has become law, he created a spiritual nationality which blended peoples of every tongue and of every race...

The idea of the unity of God proclaimed admist the exhaustion of fabulous theologies was in itself such a miracle that upon its utterance form his lips it destroyed all the ancient superstitions...

His endless prayers, his mystic conversations with God, his death and his triumph after death: all these attest not to an imposture but to a firm conviction which gave him the power to restore a dogma. This dogma was twofold, the unity of God and the immateriality of God; the former telling what God is, the latter telling what God is not...

...PHILOSOPHER, ORATOR, APOSTLE, LEGISLATOR, WARRIOR, CONQUEROR OF IDEAS, RESTORER OF RATIONAL BELIEFS, of a cult without images; the founder of twenty terrestrial empires and of one spiritual empire, that is Muhammad.

AS REGARDS ALL STANDARDS BY WHICH HUMAN GREATNESS MAY BE MEASURED, WE MAY WELL ASK, IS THERE ANY MAN GREATER THAN HE?"

Lamartine
"Historie de la Turquie", Paris 1854, Vol II

'And have We not raised high the esteem in which you, O Muhammad, are held?'
(HQ, 94:4)

'And We sent you, (O Muhammad), not but as a mercy upon all the worlds'
(HQ, 21:107)

'And Most Certainly, you, (O Muhammad) art of most sublime and exalted character.'
(HQ 68:4)

MUSLIM 'MODELS'
- HEROES AND HEROINES OF THE ISLAMIC WORLD

Prophet Muhammad (pbuh) must be our first role model, and he must also be our last. However, there are, have been, and will continue to be the great men, women and children of Islam - the Muslim Models.

After the Prophet (pbuh), his Sunnah in the form of Hadith show how the Prophets such as Moses and Jesus (may Allah be pleased with them) lived their life and they can act as our Muslim Models :

'Abraham was indeed a model, devoutly obedient to Allah, true in faith and he did not associate gods with Allah.' (HQ, 16:120)

We can look at the family of the Prophet (pbuh), his wives such as Khadija and Aisha and his daughter such as Fatima and all those good Muslims in his household. (May Allah be pleased with them)

We can look at how the Caliphs Who Took the Right Path and the Companions of the Prophet (pbuh) behaved and match their actions with the essence of the Prophet (pbuh). (May Allah be pleased with them).

Our parents, grandparents, siblings, and extended family and friends if they practice Islam for the pleasure of Allah are also Muslim Models.

The scholars of knowledge, of religion, science, art, languages, business, teach us how to live our lives using the Holy Qur'an and the Sunnah of the Prophet (pbuh). These include Imams, jurists, doctors, businessmen, artists and all those who study Islam for the pleasure of Allah.

However, there are people who have media attention, who are portraying Islam internationally in their speech and actions. They are in the fields of business, sports, politics, technology, nearly every reputable area of life. Our children emulate actors and actresses, singers, models and often the example they are presented with has no mention .of Allah. At least, our children when they switch on the television or surf through the Internet can when they see a Muslim who has attracted the attention of the international media be proud that one of their own is on the world stage and is proclaiming his thanks primarily to Allah. However, though some may have Muslim names, a Muslim Model can never be a Muslim Model unless his prime thanks is to Allah in public and private!

In the last century, there were numerous heroes and heroines in Islam in a wide variety of fields of sports, business, music, literature, religion, science, art, architecture - in fact, in every field in which mankind progresses. These are all Muslim Heroes and Heroines as reflected in the international media, and, inshallah, more of these will be created in the new Millennium and beyond.

However, there will be millions of Muslim Models whom we do not know about, the teacher, emergency relief workers, the police, the lawyers, the shop owner. Everyone has a part to play in Millennium Islam and the honours are indeed those of Paradise.

Like everything else in Islam, a balance must be achieved and limits imposed by Allah should not be transgressed. In having these Muslim 'Models', we do not want to adopt a cult of celebrity that seems to have spread the globe regarding the new film actor or pop-singer. We must pray that these Muslim Models remain good Muslims above all, and do not fall into the bad things they will be offered as successful people. A convert to Islam who had attracted the eye of the international media said:

'I may be in the back of line but at least I'm in the line. I know I have made a lot of mistakes, but I also know I have to improve. I'm not in the front but I'm there with the Muslims... I believe in Islam and I am a Muslim, alhamdullillah!'

Thus the future will create more of these Muslim Models, some who are doing well now, others not even born yet. They must be given the support and they must be taught that their main role model is Muhammad (pbuh) and that their gratitude is to the Lord of the Worlds, Allah.

THE SPHERE OF THE CALL

The Invitation to Islam - The Whole Complete Truth

There may grains of the truth, but Islam is The Truth and nothing but Truth.

Bahais - The Bahais believe that Mirza Husayn Ali was sent by God in Iran 1817 as a Prophet. They are not Muslims because Muhammad (pbuh) is the Last Prophet. Let the truth be said, for truth is very clear from falsehood - compare the characters of Muhammad (pbuh), the Last of the Prophets, the Seal of the Prophets, from all the millions of Muslim and increasingly non-Muslim accounts, with the largely unknown Mirza Husayn Ali - that is where the battle lies. Muhammad (pbuh) was, is and always will be the Proven Best Example for Mankind, and Mirza Husayn Ali appears humble in front of the attributes and achievements of Muhammad (pbuh). All Praise is due to Allah!

Buddhism - Buddhists follow the teachings of Siddhartha Gautama, who grew up in a palace in northern India in 6 BC, where he was protected from the suffering of the real world. Once he encountered this, he left the palace and reached enlightenment which led him to believe there are Four Noble Truths, which all man of reason and logic, regardless of beliefs, will have merit: 'Suffering exists; There is a reason for suffering; The way to end suffering is through the Eightfold Path. The Eightfold Path consists of Right Views, Right Thoughts, Right Speech, Right Action, Right Livelihood, Right Effort, Right Mindfulness and Right Concentration.' The belief they have of reincarnation is wrong for the fact that one can only life live best in this world, if you act as if you are on a journey with a final destination, but reincarnation means eternity in new lives. But, like Muslims, the aim is to enjoin the Right, but Forbidding of the Wrong is not mentioned. You need to know what is Right comprehensively - compare the Teachings of the Buddha the Tripitaka 'three baskets' with the Qur'an and the Sunnah of the Prophet (pbuh). Carefully look at one and then at the other. Common sense will show that the Qur'an and Sunnah of the Prophet (pbuh) can deal with every situation as if they were black and white, but the Tripitaka, even in its most modern form, does not have this comprehensiveness. This shows that Islam is the Complete and Whole Truth. Praise be to Allah!

Christianity - If the Islamic State were to be established today, look at how the Christians and Jews would be treated. This is the international accord struck by the Prophet (pbuh) as found in the charter which he granted to the Jews and Christians of Najran.

> To the Christians and the neighbouring territories, the security of God and the pledge of His Prophet are extended for their loves, their religion, and their property - to the present as walls the absent and others beside;
>
> - There shall be no interference with the practise of their faith or their observances; nor any change in their rights and privileges.
> - No bishop shall be removed from his bisphoric; nor any monk from his monastery, nor any priests form his priesthood.
> - They shall continue to enjoy everything great and small as heretofore.
> - No image or cross shall be destroyed.
> - They shall not oppress nor be oppressed.
> - They shall not practice the right so blood-vengeance as in the Days of Ignorance.
> - No taxes shall be levied from them, nor shall they be required to furnish provision for the troops

Christians are greatly divided and a religion which has been abandoned by its own intellectuals. The distorted belief of the Trinity and the Son of God just do not make sense - Islam concentrates on the Oneness of Allah (*Tauhid*). This is the version of the Prophet Jesus (may the peace of Allah be upon him) in Islam. He is the leader of the Muslims in the future, and in this Millennium. Everyone awaits his arrival, but when he arrives, as Allah has promised, will he come back as a Father-Son-Holy Spirit or as a Prophet of Allah? The truth is that he will establish the Kingdom of Allah, which will be begun by Mission Islam, established in the Islamic State by the Mahdi and where there will only be **ISLAM**.

JESUS, THE PROPHET OF ALLAH,
(May the Peace of Allah be upon him)
THE FUTURE LEADER OF THE WORLD
WHO FINALLY ESTABLISHES THE KINGDOM OF ALLAH ON EARTH

They believe that he did not have a father, and that Virgin Mary (Syeda Mariam) gave birth to Jesus through the Immaculate Conception
'She said: "O my Lord! How shall I have son when no man has touched me?"
He said: "Even so; Allah creates what He wills: when He decreed a matter, He but says to it 'BE' and it is!"' (HQ, 3:46)

Prophet Jesus (may the peace of Allah be upon him) was an apostle to the Jews saying to them
'It is Allah, Who is my Lord and your Lord; then worship Him - this is the Straight Path.' (HQ, 3:51).
He is not God: 'They disbelieved indeed those that say that Allah is Christ, the son of Mary
Say: "Who then has the least power against Allah, if His will were to destroy Christ, the son of Mary, his mother, and all - every one that is on the Earth? For to Allah belongs the dominion of the heavens and the Earth, and all that is between. He creates what He pleases. For Allah has power over all things."' (HQ 5:17)

He is not the Son of God: 'The Jews call Ezra a son of Allah, and the Christians call Christ the Son of Allah. That is saying from their mouth; (in this) they but imitate what the unbelievers of old used to say. Allah's curse be on them: how they are deluded away from the Truth!' (HQ, 9:31)

He prophesied the coming of Muhammad (pbuh): 'And remember, Jesus, the son of Mary, said "O Children of Israel! I am the Messenger of Allah (sent to you), confirming the Torah (which came) before me, and giving glad tidings of a messenger to come after me, whose name shall be Ahmad."' (HQ, 61:6)

Prophet Muhammad (pbuh) said: 'Both in this world and in the Hereafter,
I am the nearest of all the people to Isa (Jesus), the son of Maryam (Mary).
The Prophets are paternal brothers; their mothers are different, but their religion is one.'

He was not crucified, and is still alive: 'That they said (in boast), "We killed Jesus Christ, the Son of Mary, the Messenger of Allah"; but they killed him not, nor crucified him -only a resemblance of Jesus was put over another man (and they killed that man). And those who differ therein are full of doubts, with no certain knowledge but only conjecture to follow, for a surety they killed him not: No - Allah raised him up unto Himself; and Allah is Exalted in Power, Wise.' (HQ, 4:157-8)

Prophet Isa's life was incomplete; his ministry barely lasted three years; his mission was limited; and he was not called upon to deal with the many-sided problems that arise in a highly organised society or state. He is coming.

Allah's Messenger (pbuh) said: 'By Him in Whose Hand is my soul, surely Isa, the son of Maryam, will descend amongst you, and will judge mankind by the law of the Qur'an: he will break the cross and kill the pig, as Christianity will be annulled and there will be no tax taken from non-Muslims.'

EVERYONE WILL BE MUSLIM - THE KINGDOM OF ALLAH WILL BE HERE

Prophet Jesus (my Allah be pleased with him) will return after the Mahdi comes, and every sect and religion apart from Islam will be eliminated, after he has killed the Anti-Christ. Mission Islam prepares for the arrival of the Mahdi, who will be succeeded by Prophet Jesus (may Allah be pleased with him). He will lead the Islamic Earth and it will be a time of prosperity and happiness. We pray to Allah for the safe arrival of the Prophet Jesus to fulfil his Mission:

MILLENNIUM ISLAM

Hinduism - Hinduism encompasses a wife variety of beliefs in India, and is regarded as not constituting a formal religion at all. Most Hindus are polytheists - believe God takes many forms. God has three male forms, he can come to Earth as man - contrast this with Islam's simple, 'There is only One God, and He is Allah.' Hindus believe that every action, good or bad, has an effect (karma) on this life, and any righteous person will realise that every action has a reaction, good or bad. Hindus are largely embarrassed by their idols such as Ganesh, the blue elephant-headed idol, or Kalkin with a horse-head or Karrtikeya, who is six-headed, twelve-armed idol who rides a peacock - a Hindu has difficulty reconciling this religion with his modern culture. The concept of Brahmins, the highest caste in Hinduism could possibly have come from the name 'Ibrahim', as anyone can see that the roots are similar. Thus, the Hindu must realise that these are just idols, and not be ashamed of the fact that they worshipped idols. The forefathers of most people in this world were worshipping stone. Break these idols and believe in the One God, who is Allah and Allah Alone.

Jainism - The word Jain means follower of the Jinas. Jinas means 'those who overcome' as in 'those who perform a struggle', as in they have a sense of achieving discipline over one's own desires, thoughts and actions, all concepts which a Muslim believes as well as in the form of 'jihad'. There are said to be 24 Jinas, also known as Tirthankas ('bridge builders'), the last of whom was Mahavira who lived in India in the 5th century BCE. The Jains, though they incorrectly believe in reincarnation like the Buddhists and Hindus, wish to gain freedom from it, and perhaps the best way to gain freedom from reincarnation is to see whether the concept is rational or not. The belief in non-violence, ahimsa, is central to the Jain tradition, and Jains try to avoid violence to life in every form, including animals and plants as will as humans, a belief which is very peaceful. However, this is very much in the trend of enjoining the Right, and only enjoining the Right. Muslims must forbid the Wrong as well, and if Jains wish to join the Islamic State as the Jain community, it is the Muslims who will defend the Jains if they ever face oppression and persecution from another community. Thus, the Jains will learn that one must not only enjoin the good, but forbid the bad as well - the Path to Islam.

Judaism - Jews believe in one God, the Creator and Ruler of the Universe. They believe that God made a Covenant, or agreement, with Abraham/Ibrahim (maythe peace of Allah be upon him), who is regarded as the father of the Jewish people and Muslims as well. Keeping the law is the Jewish people's part in this Covenant. Jews look forward to the Messiah, a leader from God, who will bring peace, fruitfulness, and security to the whole world. Perhaps the Jews' strongest point is that the Orthodox are Unitarians and follow the laws given to Moses by God. Allah is your God. 48% live in America, 30% in Israel and 20 percent in Europe and Russia - they must realise that the religion which now encompasses the land of Moses is now Islamic - surely that is a sign that the Muslims believe that Musa (may Allah be pleased with him) was also a Prophet of Allah, but Muhammad (pbuh) is the Final Prophet of Allah. Heed the warnings:

'O Children of Israel! Remember My Favour which I bestowed upon you,
and fulfil your Covenant with me so that I fulfil My covenant with you, and fear none but Me.' (HQ, 2:40)

Muslims follow the pure monotheist religion of Abraham, as the Jews should do. However, the Jews have, according to their own history, suffered because they strayed from the Commands of Allah, as the international community has depleted. As the nearest Ummah in comparison to the Muslims, it should be easy for them to become Muslims, if they wish to. The whole Earth is Allah's, and He has bestowed His Favour upon whom He pleases. It is a historical fact that Jerusalem was only every safe under Muslims: David, Solomon, Jesus (may the peace of Allah be upon them) Muhammad (pbuh), Umar (may Allah be pleased with him), Salahuddin (may the mercy of Allah be upon him) - all are Muslims who believe in the One True God, Allah. It is the duty of every Jew to read the Holy Qur'an, for Allah has special words for the 'Children of Israel', and these will be the consequences:

'And when it is recitcd to them, they say: "We believe in it. Verily, it is the Truth from our Lord.
Indeed, even before it we have been those who submit themselves to Allah in Islam as Muslims.' (HQ, 28:53)

Muslims believe in Ibrahim's Lord, Allah, as the Jews believe in Abraham's God. How can two cousin communities believe in the same God, and then have so many differences? The answer is that someone must have more Truth than the other. The Muslims may have had the Complete Truth of Islam, but when they turned away from it, their hearts became hardened against one another, and the lost their position as the people whom Allah has bestowed His Favour upon. However, this Millennium, the Complete Truth of Islam becomes Reality.

Shintoism - Shinto is the traditional religion of Japan, and means 'the way of the gods'. Shinto religion is closely tied up with the landscape of Japan and with family ancestors. Shinto ceremonies appeal to *kami*, the mysterious powers of nature, for protection and benevolent treatment. Shinto religion follows the landscape of Japan, the family ancestors and nature - but who created all of this? It was Allah - Allah is as Powerful in Africa as He is in Japan - He Created Japan, and He Alone is Worthy of Worship.

Sikhism - In the 15th century in Punjab in India, Guru Nanak taught a new faith which sought to take the best of Hinduism and Islam and put them into a new faith called Sikhism. Sikhs believe in one God described as 'timeless and without form', creator and director of the universe. Sikhs believe that He can be found through prayer and service to others. Sikhs teachings emphasise equality, service and protection of the weak against injustice. Sikhs wear five distinctive marks of their faith, known as 'the five K's' because their names in Punjabi all begin with K.

'THE FIVE K'S' OF SIKHISM

Kesh	- Uncut hair. Devout Sikhs do not cut their hair or beard at any time.
Kanga	- a comb to keep their hair in place, kept tidy under a turban.
Kara	- a steel bangle, a complete circle symbolising one God, one truth.
Kirpan	- a small sword or dagger, a reminder of the need to fight injustice.
Kacchera	- short trousers or breeches, indicating the readiness to ride into battle.

The themes behind Sikhism are many of the Complete Path of Truth of Islam. However, Sikhism seems to be exclusively for that region in India, the Punjab, and that is where most of its adherents come from. It is largely an ethnic religion, as opposed to a universal one. Additionally, compare the character and achievements of Muhammad (pbuh) with any of the Gurus in Sikhism - the Gurus will, even when placed as one group, will appear very humble in front of the Best Example for Mankind. Sikhs must realise that Islam, as opposed to Hinduism, is the religion on which Guru Nanak based his teachings, for Islam is the Whole Complete Truth. He was largely searching for a social and religious compromise between Muslims and Hindus - no compromise was necessary, for if one is to look closely at Sikhism it just seems as if it is a distorted form of Islam, without any Hinduism, mainly for those in Punjab, India. A Sikh must realise that Islam is the foundation of their religion, which is distorted, and that they must return to the Complete Whole Truth of Islam.

Taoism - Taoism emerged in China around the first century BC, and is named after the Chinese word (Tao) (Way or Path). Tao is a natural fore, the Way of the Universe, which guides all life. Living in harmony with the Tao brings pace and harmony; struggling with it brings suffering. The balance of the universe is created by the force of yin and yang - opposite forces in continual interaction and change, giving order to all life. Yin is heavy, dark, moist and Earthy, and is associated with the feminine. Yang is airy, light, dry, hot, heavenly and associated with the masculine. Ying and Yang work in reaction to one another. Perhaps, the most famous work on the Tao is by Kung Fu Tzu (Confucius). Traditional Taoists practices include the exorcism of evil spirits and ghosts, divination in various forms, the worship of deities, many of whom have specific roles such as childbirth and illness. Taoists must realise that the Tao, the natural force, the Way of the Universe, which guides all life, is Allah and if they were to just replace the word Tao with Allah, they would soon be on their way to becoming Muslims.

Any other religion apart from Islam may have aspects of Truth, but does not have the Complete Truth. Allah has promised that in the Millennium, every religion and sect apart from Islam will be wiped out. The Mahdi will be at the apex of the Islamic State of the Millennium, and when Prophet Jesus (may the peace of Allah be upon him) arrives, then the Kingdom of Allah will finally be established. Every human will pray to Allah, and worship Allah in purity. Imagine a world where Creator and Creation come into perfect harmony - the Creator has promised that this will happen, and if He says it will happen, who are mere humans to disagree?

'Say, truth has come and falsehood has vanished, for falsehood must vanish.'
(HQ, 17:81)

THE SPHERE OF IMAGE & SUBSTANCE

'And spend of your substance in the Cause of Allah, and do not throw yourselves into destruction. But be excellent, for Allah loves those who do good with excellence.' (HQ, 2:195)

Image in Islam is everything - but only if it is backed up by substance.

Islam needs to be marketed in the way it always has been - The Truth, The Answer to the Question WHY?

Muslims can be traditional and modern, liberal and conservative, young and old, vibrant and fast, relaxed and slow, beautiful yet simple, strong yet gentle, ancient yet futuristic, for one and for all - Islam can be all these things and more provided it stays between the Laws of Allah. The utopian dream that technology could help people return to a local or clan level of communication, where common problems could be solved face to face, is still far from reality. Increasingly we realise that these technologies are mere tools and cannot solve human problems - it is only Islam that can fulfil this mission.

ISLAMIC COMMUNICATION

Talking and listening. It's how we build friendships, organise our lives, get business done, sort out problems and create new opportunities. Communication is more than just the way in which we make ourselves understood. It's how we plan and organise our lives; it's how we get close to people and build relationships; it's how we get to understand other people' points of views, add to our knowledge and create new opportunities. Above all, the ways in which we interact with others shape how others perceive and respond to us, ultimately defining what we are. You must talk and listen to each other - that is the way Islam will move forward.

THE FRIDAY SERMON

In every mosque on Friday, the sermon must be given in a style which the maximum audience of the mosque understands. There are some mosques where only Arabic will be spoken - Arabic is the Pure Language - but if the majority of your audience only speaks French well, the language of the mosque must be French. In some mosques, the often irrelevant sermon is given in Arabic first, and then in the language of the state.

This has two consequences - the first, and more minute, it leads some Muslims to improve their Arabic, if this is not their first language. The negative, and more significant, result of delivering the sermon in Arabic means that the majority of the audience does not really understand what is being said. Therefore, in all mosques, in countries where Arabic is the main language, only Qur'anic Arabic should be used throughout the sermon. After that sermon, a sermon in the language of the next highest Muslim minority who do not speak Arabic, such as English, French or Urdu should be used. In the mosques of countries where Arabic is not the main language, the sermon must first be given in the state language and once the message is understood, the same sermon in Arabic should be given.

Additionally, all Friday sermons should appeal to the rational side of man, rather than his emotions. Increasingly, in some mosques around the world, it has been felt by some members of the audience that they are being shouted AT, rather than being taught in the Sunnah of the Prophet (pbuh). The focus of the Imam should be to teach the Sunnah of the Prophet (pbuh) and cater his speech to his audience - be one of them, rather than 'above' them. Voice have been raised in mosques, with some members shouting at each other and at the audience as if they were children. As psychologists and professors of rhetoric well know, the higher the pitching and the louder the voice, the less credible the message - so lower your voice and plan and think before you speak. They must heed this proverb from Muslims in Turkey that 'Listening requires more intelligence than speaking.' However, in certain countries, where the Muslims are 'sleeping' and not following the Laws of Allah, raising and lowering the voice at times can have the desired effect of making the Muslims love their religion.

Be witty and humorous in the sermon and use words which most of the audience will understand - do not go to the other extreme and start discussing philosophy. However, contemporary and modern influences in these sermons are welcomed, and this has often been used by Imams in the West. The Holy Qur'an addresses itself to 'people who think' and 'people who understand'; those weak Muslims who like to shout a lot and create a lot of trouble should heed these words.

ISLAMIC ADVERTISING

Islam needs to be advertised in a variety of markets in a variety of ways - the words of the Holy Qur'an are the basis and the words and actions of the Prophet Muhammad (pbuh) are the best tools for this. Islam is as equally at home in a tent in central Arabia as it is in a sleek, silver skyscraper in Shanghai. The markets are different - yet the message is the same. Islam needs to be young, exciting and vibrant for the young (or young at heart) but also simple, plain and minimalist for those who like to believe in Islam in that way. The spectrum of Islam is wide enough to serve all the tastes, interests and views of those who sincerely believe that Allah is the one True God, and Muhammad is His Messenger.

ISLAMIC MARKETING

The Invitation to Islam which is sent to those living in the ghettos of Los Angeles will not be in the same style, language and format as those that are given to those living in the high-rise buildings of Sun City, South Africa - the message is the same, but the approach different. Remember one of the proverbs of the Muslims of Egypt:

' A kind welcome is better than a good dinner.'

Therefore, this is what must be done.

- Look at the market and research them - lifestyle, language, biodata such as age, history, class, wealth, background, level of education, present religion, location.
- Address them using the Words of Allah and His Prophet (pbuh) as a tool.
- Address them in their language in their style and with their words with the focus of making them embrace Islam as your number one priority.
- Incorporate knowledge and words from selected good non-Muslims and their data to support your Invitation to Islam - scrutiny is key.
- Be Moderate in your Invitation, be courteous, be wise and be gracious.
- Show the history of the world, its present and its future - their future.

ISLAMIC PUBLIC RELATIONS

Islam is, has been, but will no longer allow itself to be portrayed in a negative light, and Muslims must carry out their duties in this respect. The Prophet (pbuh) prophesied that the Arabs would become abased in the future as they are today - due to the immoral actions of some Arab Muslims and non-Muslims in the West, the stereotype has stuck. However, the Arab Muslims in their own countries are abased - they have lost the honour which they had before Islam, and which Islam strengthened.

Sadly, the clichés and stereotypes are true. Arabs and Islam are not the same and never should have been, for today it is the non-Muslim Arab who wields considerable power in Arab countries. Thus, Muslims must work to make Qur'anic Arabic, spoken and written, the most widely used language throughout the world. However, Islamic English is perhaps going to be the second most widely spoken language of communication.

It is rare for a leader to have charisma in the Islamic world today. Some of the Muslims who appear on television, in the glare of the international media, go to far lengths to make Muslims seem like the most backward in fashion, style and articulation. Some of those in international broadcasting go to extraordinary lengths to make sure that a Muslim, who is inarticulate, backward, unattractive and often shouts, rather than speaks, comes on to talk about Islamic issues, and he comes on the television just for the sake of being in the limelight, rather than for the sake of Allah. He is in most cases not a representative of the whole community, just another faction. There are those ignorant weak Muslims who talk of Islam in terms of extremes and killing the non-Muslims is often the centre of their speeches. It is a farce. Trust that this is not pure coincidence - those who dislike Islam will often interview and actually support these weak Muslims in making Islam look unattractive.

Therefore, those Muslims who are righteous, articulate, fluent, forward-looking, contemporary and care for their appearance should be allowed to talk about global Islamic issues, and communities should seek out such people to represent them and force them to occupy this position - for all these attributes are gifts from Allah to these people and must be used to implements Allah's Kingdom on Earth.

THE MILLENNIUM ISLAMIC DRESS CODE

Decency and style is the key. Allah has created man and woman in the best of forms and He wants His servants to dress decently and with style. Even if you have a lot of wealth or are poor, you must dress decently and your decency is style in itself - a poor man can have the most comfortable clothes which drape his body creating a sense of style whilst the bloated rich man with all his money cannot look that good.

We are the best of all creatures and we should dress appropriately, whilst realising that they key characteristic of Islam is modesty. Have style, dress nice, have a sense of modesty and shame and you will look beautiful:

'O Children of Adam, we have revealed to you clothing to conceal your shame and as a thing of beauty but the garment of the fear of Allah is the best of all.' (HQ, 7:26)

"Tell the believing men to lower their gaze and be mindful of their chastity ...
and tell the believing women to lower their gaze and to be mindful of their chastity." (HQ, 24:30-31)

'They should not display their beauty and ornaments except what (ordinarily) appears thereof; that they should draw their veils over their bosom and not display their beauty to their husbands...' (and those whom they can not marry) (HQ, 24.31)

In the public sphere, men and women should dress appropriately. This is where the dress code for both men and women comes in.

A woman in an abayah (a cloak which covers every part of the body except the eyes) can clearly see everything about a man if he does not conform to Islamic Fashion - she can see his body structure, his strength, his signs of virility, how handsome he is - this way she is in the advantage, and the man feels naked. An abayah is Islamic - but it degrades men who do not dress Islamically and in hot weather, if the women are wrongly forced by their husbands to wear black abayahs, they boil! The style of the abayah will change for the future - the beauty of the woman will be honoured and protected.

Millennium Islam is Islam past, present and future - the clothes that you wear should have the principles of the past but the resources of the time you are living in and the lifestyle that you live and the environment you work in. The principles are eternal - the style is dynamically eternal. Beauty and Islamic Fashion are part of the spectrum of Islam.

Nudity is forbidden. This applies to men as much as women - men are not allowed to remove their shirts in public as they liked to do so (mainly because of the lack of exercise this is an unpleasant and unintentionally hilarious scene) as much as women are not allowed to go topless. Nudity essentially makes you cheap if done in public - the more people that see you naked, the cheaper your value. You have jewels - don't give everyone the chance to handle diamonds, pearls and rubies. Only let that special person in your life see you - your spouse.

THE GUIDELINES FOR ISLAMIC CLOTHES

- Men must cover their body from navel to knees.
- Women must cover their bodies, and their hair in public. They do not have to cover their face, but if they wish to they can.
- They can wear any style of clothes, providing they are modest and protect shame.
- Women must not wear a dress which reveals the figure and arouses man's base feelings. Man must not wear clothes which reveal the masculine nature of his figure and arouses women's base feelings.
- Criteria for this includes transparent, skin-tight or revealing clothes.
- Pure silk and clothes decorated with gold are not allowed for men.
- Men are not allowed to wear women's clothing and women are not allowed to wear men's clothing.
- Muslims are not allowed to wear dress which are symbolic of other religions. They can wear clothes which are part of the Muslim culture of other regions and areas, as they are part of the Islamic Culture.

Islam encourages simplicity and modesty. Forms of dress expressing arrogance are crude and Islamically without style and unfashionable. The style of dress depends on local custom and climatic conditions. The above guidelines apply.

Millennium Islamic Fashion and Style - An Insight

Men's Hats - this does not have to be the turban, keffiyah or fez of the past - it can be a sleek, silver-coloured type super-plastic which fits over the contours of your hair managing your hair, shampooing and conditioning it before your date with the wife!

Women should cover their hair in public - this does not have to be a piece of cloth, like a hijab or abayah - the future could mean that your hair is covered by anything be it a superflexible plastic sheet which is connected to each strand of your hair but does not allow your hair to be seen. This way you can feel that your hair is out and you feel attractive, but men who gaze at you unlawfully will not get the thrill that your husband does at home!

Men's and Women's Clothes - they do not have to be the thob, jalabiya, shalwar kameez or business suit of the past, but the thob, shalwar kameez and suit of the future which can be modified for life in the Millennium. The more akin it is to the spirit of Islam, the better it is. Additionally, colour will matter as well depending on your location on the Earth. Black and dark colours are difficult to wear in Mecca because they absorb heat, and therefore white and pastel colours should be worn. Therefore, Millennium Islamic Fashion requires Muslims to think before they dress.

THE STYLE THAT ROCKS THE EARTH: ISLAMIC STYLE

THE SPHERE OF WOMAN

'Whoever performs good deeds, whether male or female, and is a believer,
We shall make them live a good life and
We will certainly reward them for the best for what they did.'
(HQ, 16:97)

'At the end of the millennium, women in the world (almost 2.47 billion) are living in widely differing situations in terms of material wealth. However, what they all have in common is that they hold the most unfavourable positions, and that they are involved in constant and diverse battles in the quest for greater equality.'

Women and Men are equal in Islam, but women have been the brunt of too much negativity thorough history - this will help to readdress this negativity.

ISLAM - THE RELIGION WHICH REVERES THE LADY

Throughout history, men and woman have never been treated the same. Islam has given women the right position, and has not violated Divine laws. Other religions and philosophies have been unable to visualise the exact and right role of women until today. In the West, women have been reduced almost to a commodity of enjoyment and fancy. And women have tended to degrade themselves unwittingly in modern times, for in the name of equality, they have become the objects of exploitation by men, and the slogans of liberty and equality have virtually reduced them to playful commodities. They have neither gained liberty nor achieved equality, rather they have lost their roles as Queen of the Home.

Emasculation (cutting the virility of men) and feminisation of non-Muslim society has taken place whereas in the Islamic world, misogyny (subordination of women) has occurred. Total opposites - which means that a balance has to be made and, like in any situation, Islam is the solution. Men and women are partners created for the sake of one another - and because of this they have differences. An average man is stronger, heavier, harder in muscles and taller than an average woman. Women can become pregnant and bear children, men cannot. Women tend to be sensitive, emotional and tender while men are comparatively less emotional and more practical. The differences are cause for celebration in Islam, not anger and strife.

In the West, women have taken greater roles and become professional and compete for jobs with men whereas men are angry and vulnerable at being forced to abandon their masculinity in a variety of ways - such as dangerous sports. The solution is that the men become Muslims and are then part of a culture which makes Man responsible for the protection and maintenance of Woman. The career women are finding that they have sold their life for a job when they have lost the joy to have children - one of the best joys in life - thus they become Muslims and start raising more Muslims and also continue their career, but in a career where they do not have to compete with men and where the inherent attributes that Allah has given women are used to their optimum.

In the Islam world, the Millennium will be a time when women in the world will be given the true rights and privileges they were given back in the seventh century by the Prophet (pbuh) and which are applicable for all time. Just because some regimes have not given women these rights and privileges as a whole for centuries, does not mean that they have vanished. These rights and privileges have been given to women by Allah, the All-Knowing Creator, and no man or woman has the right to take these away. The Holy Qur'an shows that women have the freedom to express their opinion and to gain their Islamic rights. Women in the time of the Prophet (pbuh) enjoyed this right, and not only did they express their opinions freely, but even debated and participated in serious discussion with the Prophet (pbuh) himself and with other Muslims of the time.

'It's a Man's World, but it would be nothing without a Woman'.

How true. Therefore, the role of Muslim women in the future, is, as it was in the time of the Prophet (pbuh) - as dynamic, vibrant, pious, beautiful, noble, excellent women. The prime role of a woman in Islam is as a Muslim, and then as mother and as a wife. To see how she performs in the Hereafter, and whether He grants her entry into the Paradise of Firdaus, is how pious she is, and then after that how good a wife and mother she is. For a woman, piety goes together with being a good wife and good mother.

Let us look at what the Best Example for Mankind, Prophet Muhammad (pbuh) said about women:

AS MOTHERS

'Paradise lies at the feet of your mothers.'

Once a person asked the Prophet (pbuh), **'Who deserves the best care from me?'**
The Prophet (pbuh) replied **'Your mother (he repeated three times), then your father and then your nearest relatives.'**

AS A WIFE

'The best among you is the one who is the best towards his wife.'

'O people, your wives have certain rights over you and you have certain rights over them. Treat them well and be kind to them, for they are your partners and committed helpers.'

<u>**ISLAM**</u> PUTS WOMAN ON AN **EQUAL FOOTING** WITH MAN - THEY ARE **PARTNERS - 50/50**

However, we must be honest - weak Muslim governments of the past and rulers have been unIslamic in practice in terms of law towards women, and that is why so many of them feel so angry. That is why we see a feminisation of society, and an emasculation of society. We do not need either of these. We want honour, nobility and love, a masculine and feminine culture built on Islam.

Over fourteen centuries ago, Islam granted women the rights to their own property, to choose their own partners, divorce, abortion when necessary (such as rape), education and sexual satisfaction in marriage - this can only lead to one conclusion - MUSLIM WOMEN HAVE BEEN CHEATED! Therefore, Muslim women must work with good righteous Muslim men who know the Truth and DEMAND these rights back. When a woman wants to divorce her husband, because he is primarily a bad man, or an adulterer or a murderer, she should be allowed to. Muslim women must fight for these basic rights and there are men out there, good Muslims, who will help you in your battle to gain your rights - centuries old.

A WOMAN IN THE FUTURE IS THE BEST WOMAN
IF SHE HAS ALL THE RIGHTS THAT ISLAM GAVE HER AND SHE TRIES TO BE
PIOUS, BEAUTIFUL, INTELLIGENT, RICH AND HONOURABLE

Islam is the liberator of the woman -
it gives them the freedom which they need and the rights, responsibilities and duties
which they can use to live their life to the optimum. No Muslim woman will be oppressed in the future when
Islamic Law is established - this is the Promise of Allah and His Messenger

**'Verily, the Muslims, men and women, the believers, men and women,
the obedient men and women, the truthful men and women,
the patient men and women, the men and women who are humble before their Lord,
the charitable men and women who give charity, (Zakah and Sadaqah)
The men and women who observe fasting, the men and women who guard their chastity, and
the men and women who remember Allah much with their hearts and tongues -
Allah has prepared for them forgiveness and a great reward.'** (HQ, 33:35)

ISLAMIC RIGHTS OF THE MUSLIM WOMAN

YOUR OWN PERSON & IDENTITY

Women have a separate and distinct identity - the right to own property, the owner of her earnings which no-one has a right over except her. She can dispose of her earnings and property as she wishes, but only in righteous means and towards righteous ends.

INHERITANCE

She has the right to inheritance.
'She has a part in the property of her dead father, husband or childless brother (HQ, 4:7, 32, 176).

CHOOSE YOUR MUSLIM HUSBAND

She has a right to choose her husband. No one can impose a decision on her against her will. She has a right to divorce her husband if their marriage becomes impossible to sustain.
Muslim men should marry Muslim women, numbering up to four at one time.
Muslim women are only allowed to marry Muslim men.

CHASTITY IS YOUR RIGHT

'If any man falsely questions a woman's chastity, that man is declared unfit for giving evidence.' (HQ, 24:4). If she is chaste, no truly Islamic court on Earth will allow her chastity to be questioned.
A woman's honour in Islam is safeguarded from false accusations.

ENJOY A RIGHTEOUS CAREER

A woman has the right to develop her talents in a righteous way and to work for the spectrum of Islam. She was given the right by the Holy Qur'an to earn a living and to enjoy the proceeds as an independent individual: 'For men, there is reward for what they have earned, and likewise for women, there is a reward for what they have earned. And ask Allah of His Bounty - surely, Allah is He Who knows Everything.' (HQ, 4:32)

ENJOY SEX IN MARRIAGE

A woman has the right to enjoy lawful sex with her husband and be satisfied.

ISLAMIC DUTIES OF A WOMAN IN ISLAM

THE FIVE PILLARS

She must practice all the five pillars of Islam.
She is exempted from Salah and Sawm during her period. Friday prayer is optional for women.

THE QUEEN OF THE FAMILY

It is her duty to bring up children according to the needs of Islam.
She has to look after the family and has almost absolute control over domestic affairs, although the family is run by mutual consultation and co-operation.

DRESS MODESTLY

She should dress modestly in public.

PARTNERS IN LOVE

She is her husband's partner, friend, companion, lover, confidante and the husband her's.
A faithful wife is like a garment - a source of peace, happiness and contentment for her husband.

BE CHASTE

She is required to maintain her chastity at all times

OBEY THE COMMANDS

If she is asked to defy the commands of Allah,
she must defy her husband, her father, her brother, everyone.

THE SPHERE OF MARRIAGE AND FAMILY

'Men are the protectors and maintainers of women,
because Allah has given the one more (strength) than the other,
and because they support them from their means.
Therefore, the righteous women are devoutly obedient,
and guard in the husband's absence what Allah would have them guard.' (HQ, 4:34)

The Holy Qur'an calls man and woman a garment for each other, signifying their reciprocal closeness to each other. What is physically and continuous closer to oneself than ones' clothing? Marriage is a sacred institution, where man and woman combine as the pair Allah created to bring joy to the world.

Though it has been the case that monogamy has been the most dominant type of life amongst Muslims, too many rule out the bliss and joy that can be enjoyed by having up to four wives and that is what the future will show. There are strength and virtuous in a polygamous marriage as there are in a monogamous one, and it was Muhammad's (pbuh) destiny to demonstrate both in their perfection.

MONOGAMY & POLYGAMY IN ISLAM

The Prophet (pbuh) said 'Women are men's partners.'

The Prophet (pbuh) said **'Whoever Allah grants him a righteous woman has got HALF his religion. Thus, he should fear Allah in the other half.'**

All Muslims must remember that Allah has made polygamy and monogamy legal - the Muslims have been imitating the West in the regard of strict monogamy without realising that it was the Roman and Pagan jurist, Emperor Justinian, who made monogamy a matter of legislation in Europe. There are more woman on the planet than there are men, and the number is going to rise. Rather than have people alone, or becoming sexual deviants, marriage to more than one woman is possible and lawful as Allah has said so. Polygamy is practiced in Islam in special circumstances and one of those is when a society has more women than men. This especially happens after war. The Verse in the Holy Qur'an allowing more than one wife was revealed after the battle of Uhud in which many Muslim men were martyred. Today, there are more women than men.

'Marry women of your choice, two, or three, or four;
But if you fear that ye shall not be able to deal justly (with them),
Then only one,
or that which your right hand possesses,
that will be more suitable to prevent you doing any injustice.'
(HQ, 4:3)

'It is not lawful for you (to marry more) women after this not to change them for other wives,
even though their beauty attract you, except any your right hand possess (as handmaidens):
and Allah has control over all things.'
(HQ, 33.52)

Women around the world want to have a career, education, children and a great husband - they want it all.
They can have it all.

Imagine a scene where four women are married to one man. He spends one night with each of them. They can be independent women, with their own lives, property, businesses but they will have children with this one man who has to treat them justly. The four women can be friends, and as Muslim women they must learn to respect and love one another as a fellow Muslim who obeys Allah. However, man must remember that he must be just towards his wives. The concept of jealousy is inevitable - when one of the wives of the Prophet (pbuh) said that she would be jealous, he said that he would pray to Allah for her not to be. The man and his wives must all have a loving and affectionate marriage. How many women are looking for Mr. Right but find he is married - in Islam that would not matter, if his first wives did not object to the marriage, you could be another one of your Mr. Right's wives! If you are a man and feel that you could never be faithful to one woman and fear committing adultery because you love this other woman as well, then marry her! Allah gives a man the power to love - he has said that a man can have enough love for four women at once - and he can also have love for the children and for his friends and family! Absence for those three nights will make the woman realise that absence does make the heart fonder!

The Prophet (pbuh) said 'Marry a woman who is affectionate and fertile,
for I will boast over all nations concerning your number.'

A woman who is going to be a second wife could refuse to marry the man on the grounds that he already has a wife. But if a woman happily consents to her husband marrying again and the second wife agrees, why should anyone else object to it? However, all Muslim men who wish to have a polygamous marriage must realise that it takes a special man to maintain, protect and love four women and to treat them justly - only if you believe you have this special quality should you consider polygamy. If this is done for lust as the primary motive, the consequences are very harmful to society - so realise that this is a commitment to Allah as well.

'You will NEVER be able to do PERFECT justice between wives even if it is your ardent desire, so do not incline to much to one of them as to leave the other hanging.
And if YOU DO JUSTICE, and DO all that is right and fear Allah by keeping away from all that is wrong, then Allah Is Ever Oft-forgiving, Most Merciful.' (HQ, 4:129)

The Prophet (pbuh) said 'A woman is married for four reasons: her wealth, lineage, beauty and religion.
You better marry the righteous woman or you'll lose.'

ONLY ONE HUSBAND

Polyandry is when a woman has more than one husband is forbidden in Islam. This is an evident matter. It is impractical and it creates more problems than it solves. How will paternity be decided? Which husband would claim fatherhood over the child - the one who raises him or his biological father? How would inheritance be decided? Such questions have no answer in polyandry. Moreover, it is possible for man to live with more than one wife and have children from all of them, but for a woman to please more than one husband seems almost impossible. A woman can bear children from only one husband in marriage. That is why polyandry is forbidden in Islam.

NO BOYFRIENDS OR GIRLFRIENDS - ONLY MARRIAGE

Neither is the concept of boyfriend or girlfriend allowed in Islam - this has led to all sorts of problems, and the only solution is that the those who are able to marry, when they reach a certain age, and have sexual desires, should be married - the minimum age of this should be fifteen, when education is at its minimum acceptable level and when sexual desires are too prominent for many to control. All Muslims, parents and children and adolescents who fear committing acts outside Islam should heed the words of the Prophet (pbuh):

'**O youth, he who is physically able to marry, let him marry. It is best for lowering the gaze, more protective of chastity, and he who cannot, let him fast**.'

**'O you who believe! Why do you prohibit the good which Allah has legalised for you?
Do not transgress. Verily, Allah does not like the transgressors.'**
(HQ, 5:87)

HE SHOWED THE EXCELLENCE OF BOTH

Thus whether you are a monogamous man or woman or a polygamous man or a woman who feels she could be part of a polygamous marriage, The Holy Qur'an and the Way of the Prophet (pbuh) still remain your best evidence. For monogamy, see the bliss and love that Muhammad (pbuh) had with Khadija. For polygamy, see the bliss and love that Muhammad had with his numerous wives during their marriage such as Aisha and Umm Salama (may Allah be pleased with them all).

A MARRIAGE MADE IN HEAVEN

Aisha (may Allah be pleased with her) said 'Once I travelled with Allah's Messenger (pbuh) when I was young and not plump. Then, he asked, his Companions to go forward and they did so. Afterwards he said, "Let us race each other." Therefore, I started to run until I won. Later on when I became plump and forgot what had happened, I travelled with him again. He asked his Companions to go forward again and they did so. Then, he said, "Let us race each other. I had forgotten what had happened in the first race. I was plump, therefore I said, "Messenger of Allah, how can I race you in this state?" However, he said, "Let us race." Then, he won the race. He started to laugh and said, "This was the opposite of the last one."'

'One day, the Prophet (pbuh) asked me,
"What are these?" "My dolls," I replied.
"What is this in the middle?" he asked. "A horse," I replied.
"And what are these things on it?" he asked. "Wings," I said.
"A horse with wings?" he said.
"Have you not heard that Solomon, the son of David, had horses with wings?" I said.
Thereupon, the Messenger of Allah (pbuh) laughed so heartily that I could see his molars.

'The Messenger of Allah (pbuh) would say to Aisha (may Allah be pleased with her)
'I know when you become angry or pleased with me.'
She asked 'How could you know that?'
He said **'When you are pleased, you say, "No, by the Lord of Muhammad"**
and when you are angry you say, "No, by the Lord of Ibrahim!"'
Thereupon, she said **'Yes, but by Allah, O Allah's Messenger, I leave nothing but your name.'**

The Prophet (pbuh) said '**When the husband and wife hold each other's hands, Allah forgives their sins**.'

The Prophet (pbuh) said **'What I like most of your world is three things:**
women, perfume, and prayer, which is the dearest thing to my eye.'

PARADISE

The Prophet (pbuh) said
'The believer will have a tent of a vacuum pearl, the length of which is thirty miles.
He will also have wives with whom he has sexual intercourse, yet they never met one another.'

The Prophet (pbuh) said 'In Paradise, the believer will be provided with sexual ability equal to such and such.'
Anas asked, 'Could he endure that, Messenger of Allah?'
The Prophet (pbuh) said, '**He will be as strong as a hundred**.'

Abu Hurairah (may Allah be pleased with him) asked the Messenger of Allah (pbuh)
'Messenger of Allah! Will we approach our wives in Paradise?"'
The Prophet (pbuh) answered **'The man will approach a hundred virgins a day.'**

Laqit Al-'Aquily asked 'Messenger of Allah! Will we have righteous wives in Paradise?'
He said 'Righteous men are for righteous women. You will give pleasure to each other without childbirth.'

Abu Hurairah (may Allah be pleased with him) asked the Prophet (pbuh)
"Will we have sexual intercourse in Paradise?'
The Prophet (pbuh) answered 'By Him in Whose Hand is my soul! It will be very tense.
Yet as soon as he has finished, she returns to a virgin again.'

The Prophet (pbuh) said
'No sooner do the people of Paradise have sexual intercourse with their wives,
then the wives become virgins again.'

Oral sex

The distinguishing factor of the Islamic Ummah among the other peoples is that it is the religion of shame and modesty. The act of oral sex is diametrically opposed to this important Islamic injunction of modesty. The face and mouth fulfils a very important function in the human body. It is the pathway for the recitation of the Holy Qur'an and the Remembrance of Allah (*dhikr*). Due to this factor, cleaning the mouth with a toothbrush or miswak is very important for this function, The angels draw close and touch the lips of the reciter of the Holy Qur'an with their lips. The mouth must not be abused and defied for the mean act of oral sex.

Intercourse during menstruation

The Holy Qur'an has emphatically prohibited sexual intercourse during menstruation: (HQ, 2:222) However, sexual activity, as long as no sexual intercourse takes place, is permitted, for when the Prophet (pbuh) wanted to do something with one of his wives during their menstrual period, he covered her vagina and did what he wanted.

Husband's/Wife's refusal for sex

If a husband/ wife wants to fulfil their sexual urges in a halal fashion, and the respective partner refuses to fulfil these urges, then they are a disobedient husband/ wife in Islam. The husband must have sex with his wife if she wants to fulfil her urges in a halal fashion, and the wife must have sex with her husband if he wants to fulfil his urges in a halal fashion. The Prophet (pbuh) said 'If the husband calls her to bed and she refused causing his displeasure and anger, then the angels rain curses upon her for the duration of the nigh until daybreak.'

A HUSBAND / WIFE CAN ONLY REFUSE TO HAVE SEX IF WHAT THEY ARE BEING ASKED TO DO DISOBEYS ALLAH AND IS HARAAM OR IF THEY ARE ILL.

If the husband says to indulge in some haraam sex for example, the wife must say no. If the wife says to indulge in some haraam sex, the husband must say no. Don't refuse the urges of the other partner if they want to have sex in a halal way - have halal sex.

SEXUAL POWER

Sexual power varies from individual to individual. Some men are virile while others are not. However, on an overall basis, women are said to have a greater desire than men but this has been concealed within the shroud of natural modesty that is the inherent trait within women. It is for this reason that shame (*haya*) is regarded as a vital quality for women. Minus this quality, she is prone to committing many promiscuous deeds. Once she has lost this quality of modesty, she is capable of committing the most shameless of deeds.

SEXUAL POTENCY

Allah gives Muslims much greater sexual potency than non-Muslims because they worship Him and sincerely seek His help. The Prophet (pbuh) told Ali (may Allah be pleased with him) to have eggs to increase his sexual potency. Additionally, Archangel Jibril told the Prophet (pbuh) to eat *Harisa*, a kind of thick soup made of crushed wheat, pieces of meat, butter, certain spices, etc. for THE POTENCY OF 40 MEN. Eat these foods for potency - grains, vegetables, fruits, nuts, meat, dairy products, spices and Avoid these if you do not want more sexual potency - all sour foods, tamarind, pickles, red chillies, aniseed, caffeine, sour fruits, chutneys, vinegar, hot spices, tea, coffee.

The Prophet (pbuh) said **'The halal is clear and the haram is clear and in between them are ambivalent matters which many people do not know. Whomever guards himself against ambivalent matters has secured his faith and his honour. Whoever falls in ambivalent matters will fall into the haram is like the shepherd who shepherds (his flock) around forbidden pastures.'**

A brief introduction into the treasures of Islamic knowledge for an attractive man or woman with a good knowledge on how to have. You have knowledge now on how to please your spouses and yourselves. Use it wisely and may Allah grant you a PROSPEROUS, SEXY, HAPPY MARRIED LIFE.

THE HEART - THE ESSENCE

If you want to be an achiever in the Millennium, you must have hope and be optimistic. The only hope that really helps is that Allah is the One True God. Everything else comes from there. It is time to take control of your lives, like a special event in your lives. All it takes is one day to decide what you want to be. Think and focus about who you are, where you have been and where you are going and then ACT - establish the Kingdom of Allah on Earth.

THOSE WITHOUT HOPE - THE PESSIMISTS

'Those who reject the Signs of Allah and the Meeting with Him - it is they who shall despair of My Mercy and it is they who suffer a most painful torment.' (HQ, 29:23)

The pessimist conveys to those around him a loss of faith not merely in himself but in life. Such a person is no great joy to be around. People avoid the pessimist. He ends up in a self-created state of solitary confinement, his constant paranoia about the lonely condition of man confirmed. Social isolation and loneliness in turn breed despair, physical ill-health and psychological problems. The pessimists often are dissatisfied with life and this makes them hurt themselves and their bodies, through excess in everything bad, such as drugs and alcohol to make up for their lack of hope. They believe in nihilism - destroying themselves and in fatalism - that they will fail and lose. They believe things will not only get worse, but that there is nothing or no one to stop it. They blame external forces when things go wrong. Einstein observed that the tragedy of life was what dies inside a man while he lives. It is hope that dies - the belief that things can, and will, get better.

'On the Day when the Hour will come, the guilty will be plunged in destruction with despair.' (HQ, 30:12)

THOSE WITH FAITH AND HOPE - THE OPTIMISTS

Optimism is good for you. An optimist tends to have a greater satisfaction in relationships, and less conflict. The optimist often has the highest quality of life, enjoying better physical health, coping more constructively with illness and recovering more speedily. An optimistic frame of mind makes the immune system stronger and enables you able to cope with and destroy stress and physical diseases. Not only do high self-esteem and a sense of personal control give rise to good health, but they increase the amount and quality of social relationships. Thus, optimists are attractive people to be around and they are naturally therefore less likely to become depressed, or make others depressed.

An optimist is not an optimist because they have suffered less - rather it is optimism which enhances satisfaction with life. Life may not be going well, but the optimist still believes that something good will come - you just need to be patient and have trust. Optimists tend to take control of their lives and self-evaluate - they know the basic strengths and flaws of themselves and the situations they are involved in. Even in the most deprived and poor areas of the world, you will find great faith and hope - that the situation can, and will, get better.

Those who strive at the frontiers of scientific research, who struggle to bring about a more fair economic global system, those who strive for justice in their daily lives, those who were driven from their homes in persecution and whose families were killed because of mere labels were, and are, optimists. They have declared their faith in the incredible redemptive qualities which are inherent in every human. Optimists are realists - it may be a case of one struggle after another, but they know that you have to just keep going. There will be light at the end of the tunnel. Striving that extra distance can make all the difference.

The optimist is a Muslim, and an optimist can only be someone who believes in God, and the One True God is Allah. He is the Lord of All the Worlds, and He wants all of mankind, not just the Muslims, to believe in Him. However, it is the Muslims whom He has given the gift of being those who struggle in His Name, who perform the intellectual, spiritual and defensive jihad in His Way. Look at what it means to be someone without belief in Allah - you must, should and will believe in Him and practice His Religion.

THE OPTIMISTS ARE THE PLAYERS OF THE MILLENNIUM - MUSLIMS
HOPE, TRUTH, JUSTICE, FREEDOM, JIHAD = P A R A D I S E

The Prophet (pbuh) said:

'Truly, Allah will raise up at the beginning of every century for this people, one who will renew their religion for them.'

'Who so pays respect to a reprehensible innovator in Islam, he has helped in the demolition of the foundations of Islam.'

'Whoever introduces into this affair of ours that which is not of it, then it is rejected.'

'Islam was alien amongst the people in the beginning and soon it will again become strange to the people. So glad tidings be to those strangers who will rise to correct the religion of Allah whose image had been destroyed and driven away from my Way.'

'Knowledge is acquired and imparted to others not for any monetary compensation but for the good of society, and also merely for the pleasure of Allah.'

The good friends said:

Esposito said '**They are indeed the trailblazers or architects of contemporary Islamic revivalism, men whose ideas and methods have been studied and emulated from the Sudan to Indonesia.**"

Voll said '**Dynamism in the Muslim World is nothing new, and renovators of Islam have been making sure that the Straight Path remains start. Renewal (*tajdid*), reform (*islah*), authenticity (*asala*) and renaissance (*nadha*) were common themes and are common themes throughout the Muslim World**.'

Esposito said '**Muslim revivalists insist that the current religious revival is not simply a reaction to the West, but rather that it is part of an ongoing process of revival (*tajdid*) and reform (*islah*) which reflects a continuing tradition in Islamic history. John O. Voll in 'Renewal and Reform in Islamic History' maintains that central to the process of renewal in Islam is the revivalist call for a return to the fundamentals of Islam. However, the meaning and method varies with changing historical circumstances. What emerges is the picture of a tradition which, although fixed and stable, is neither stagnant nor monolithic. When the existing conditions and institutions of Islam seemed to warrant it, Muslim reformers have felt free to challenge the blind following of tradition (*taqlid*) and the Islamic establishment. They claimed their right to engage in independent analysis and interpretation (*Ijtihad*) in order to reform their societies**.'

The Cambridge Illustrated History of the Islamic World states

'**In future the Muslims world is likely to be even more powerfully engaged with outside forces and more fully shaped by its interaction with them. The contemporary Muslim community forms a world community whose diaspora is in constant contact with the heartland. New electronic means of contact, telephones, fax machines, satellite television, the Internet, make possible the exchange of ideas and culture with unprecedented speed and intensity. This exchange, moreover, is unlikely to be halted for long by the rising influence of Islamist movements; that is checked by the Shariah, as Basim Musallam has shown, at the threshold to the Muslim home. Islamists can drive alien influence out of public sphere, but their ability to prevent them from affecting domestic space is limited.**

History demonstrated the capacity of Muslims to contribute to many cultures in creating a remarkable human achievement. In doing so, they have stored up riches not just for themselves but for all humankind.

A constant source of inspiration, as this volume has endeavoured to show, has been the Qur'an, the life of the Prophet, and the moral vision which they offer human beings and their communities. In this vision and in their achievement lie our hopes for the Muslim future.'

The irony:

William Montgomery Watt writing on the woeful state of the modern Islamic world:

'Out of all this ferment something may yet come.

It is far too soon to pronounce this situation hopeless.

A man with the requisite training, and above all the gifts of courage and wisdom, might transform the whole scene.

It is practically certain that he would meet with fierce criticism from his colleagues, and would have to stand firm.

His opponents might also have to resort to violence.

He would therefore have to have sufficient personal magnetism to gain the support of the masses and a proportion of the elite.

Where is such a man to be found?'

The Truth:

"Say, truth has come and falsehood has vanished,
for falsehood must vanish."
(HQ, 17:81)

'Verily, Allah commands justice,
and performing good deeds with excellence,
and giving help to kith and kin,
and He forbids all evil deeds and oppression.
He admonishes you, so that you may take heed.'
(HQ, 16:90)

THERE IS NO GOD BUT ALLAH, THE MOST COMPASSIONATE, THE MOST MERCIFUL AND MUHAMMAD IS HIS MESSENGER

THE ISLAMIC CITY

THE ISLAMIC WORLD

THE ISLAMIC SPACE

THE ISLAMIC UNIVERSE

THE DESTINATION ISLAM

THE ISLAMIC METROPOLIS

THE ISLAMIC MATRIX

THE ETERNAL BATTLE OF GOOD VS EVIL:
MAN VS HIMSELF

FEEL THE ISLAMIC FORCE

TRUTH, JUSTICE & THE ISLAMIC WAY

CHOOSE LIFE HERE AND IN THE HEREAFTER:
CHOOSE ISLAM

THERE CAN ONLY BE ONE ALLAH
THERE CAN ONLY BE ONE ISLAM

THE MIND IS THE FORTRESS
ISLAM

GATEWAY TO THE FUTURE:
ISLAM

ISLAM SUPREME

BE AND IT IS

WELCOME TO THE ISLAMIC PARADISE

THE ISLAMIC UTOPIA

THE IDEA IN IDEAL: ISLAM

FILM WITH 'ILM : ISLAM

ILM ISLAMIC LIGHT MUHAMMAD

LET ME HELP YOU: ISLAM

I CAN ONLY SHOW YOU THE DOOR:
YOU HAVE TO OPEN IT

NO MAN, NO LAW, NOR WAR CAN STOP
ISLAM

THE UNITED STATES OF ISLAM

ICOM - THE ISLAMIC CONFEDERATION OF
MUSLIMS

HE IS COMING
WELCOME TO THE LAND
OF THE FREE & BRAVE:
WELCOME TO ISLAM

PLANET ISLAM

THE MAXIMUM FORCE OF THE FUTURE:
ISLAM

YOUR ASSIGNMENT
SHOULD YOU CHOOSE TO ACCEPT IT:
ISLAM

BEYOND WAR, THERE IS PEACE.
ISLAM

MUHAMMAD:
YOU'LL BELIEVE A MAN IS THE BEST

THERE IS NO SUBSTITUTE:
ISLAM

IN THE NOT TOO DISTANT FUTURE,
WARS WILL NO LONGER EXIST.
THERE WILL BE ISLAM

THE FUTURE IS HERE:
ISLAM

WITH GREAT POWER
COMES GREAT RESPONSIBILITY:
ISLAM

WHY?
ISLAM

THE KINGDOM OF ALLAH

OUR LORD,
GRANT US THE BEST OF THIS WORLD
& THE BEST OF THE HEREAFTER
AND PROTECT US FROM
THE TORMENT OF THE FIRE

COURAGE,
SPEED,
BEAUTY,
STRENGTH,
INTELLIGENCE,
HONOUR

THE BLESSINGS OF ALLAH, THE KING

BIBLIOGRAPHY

All scholarly work has been utilised in aim to work towards the creation of the Kingdom of Allah. May Allah reward all those involved in this world and in the Hereafter. Every effort has been made for authenticity, but only the Holy Qur'an remains without error.

- *The Holy Qur'an* (English translation of the meanings and Commentary), Printing Complex for The Holy Qur'an, Al-Madinah Al-Munawarah, 1413 (1994)
- *The Noble Qur'an* (English Language), Darusalaam, Al-Madinah Al-Munawarah, 1996
- *The World Guide 1999/ 2000 - MILLENNIUM EDITION*, New Internationalist Publications, Oxford
- *The Hutchinson Almanac 1999 - The new Almanac for the new Millennium*, Helicon, London 1999
- Foud Al-Farsy, *Saudi Arabia - A Case Study in Development*, Routeledge, UK 1986
- Ismail R. Al-Faruqi, *Islam*, Argus Communications, USA 1979
- Lamya Al-Faruqi, *Women, Muslim Society & Islam*, American Trust Publications 1998
- Imam an-Nawawi, *The Complete Forty Hadith*, Ta-ha Publishers, London 1998
- Dr. 'Abdullah 'Abdurahman Al-Shimemeri, *Descriptions of Hell from the Qur'an and Hadeeth*, Abul-Qasim Publishing House, Jeddah, Saudi Arabia 1990
- Akbar S. Ahmed, *Discovering Islam - Making Sense of Muslim History and Society*, Routeledge, London 1988
- Waseef Ahmed Ansari, *Reflections of the Blueprint of Islamic State in the Holy Quran*, International Islamic Publishers, Karachi 1989
- Muhammad ibn 'Izzat Muhammad 'Arif, *Al Mahdi and the End of Time*, (Translation by Aisha Bewley), Dar Al Taqwa, London 1997
- Muhammad Asad, *Sahih Al-Bukhari - The Early Years of Islam*, Dar Al-Andalus, Gibraltar, 1938
- Mustafa Ashour, *The Jinn in the Qur'an and the Sunna*, (Translation by Aisha Bewley), Dar Al Taqwa Ltd., London 1989
- Sheikh 'Alee Hasan 'Alee 'Abdul Hameed, *Paradise: Its Blessings and the Path to it* (Translation by Mrs. Huda Khattab), Dar Al Taqwa, 1995
- Zubair Ismail Bayat, *Etiquettes of Sexual Relations - Important Islamic Guidance for Husband and Wife*. Mahmoodiyya Publications, South Africa 1995
- Zakaria Bashier, *Sunshine at Medina*, The Islamic Foundation UK 1990
- M. Bleher, *The New Millennium through Muslim Eyes*, UKIM, Birmingham 1999
- Titus Burckhardt, *Art of Islam - Language and Meaning*, World of Islam Festival Trust, UK 1976
- Michael Dillon, *China's Muslims,* Oxford University Press, Oxford 1996
- John L. Esposito, *The Islamic Threat - Myth or Reality?*, Oxford University Press, Oxford 1992
- (Ed.) John. L. Esposito.*Voices of Resurgent Islam,* Oxford University Press, Oxford 1983.
- (Ed.) Martin Frishman and Hasan-uddin Khan, *The Mosque - History, Architectural Development & Regional Diversity*, Thomas and Hudson, London 1994
- Fethullah Gulen, *Questions this Modern Age puts to Islam*, Truestar, UK 1995
- Fethullah Gulen, *Prophet Muhammad as COMMANDER*, Truestar, UK1996
- Muhammad Husayn Haykal, *The Life of Muhammad*, (Translation by Isma'il Ragi A. al Faruqi), Centre of Islamic Studies, Qum 1976
- Murad Hofmann, *Islam 2000*, Amana Publications, Maryland, USA 1996
- Akhlaq Hussain, *Prophet's Guidance for Social Life*, International Islamic Publishers, Karachi 1984
- Ibn Kathir, *The Signs before the Day of Judgment*, (Translation by Mrs Huda Khattab) Dar Al Taqwa Ltd., London 1991
- Dr. Mohammed Khalifa, *The Sublime Quran and Orientalism*, International Islamic Publishers, Karachi 1989
- Dr. Mustafa Mahmoud, *Muhammad - His Life, His Miracles, With His Companions*, (Translation by Niemat Ali Gadalla), Dar Al Taqwa, London 1997
- (Ed.) George Mitchell, *Architecture of The Islamic World - Its History and Social Meaning*, Thomas and Hudson, London 1978
- Muslim Directory, *Muslim Directory 2000*, Blackmore Press, London 2000
- Said Nuseibeh and Oleg Grabar, *The Dome of the Rock*, Thomas and Hudson, London 1996
- David Musa Pidcock, *Satanic Voices - Modern and Ancient*, Mustaqim, Milton Keynes, 1992
- Dr. Abdul Rauf, *Illustrated History of Islam*, Ferozsons, Pakistan 1993

- Dr. Abdul Rauf, *Illustrated Stories from the Qur'an*, Ferozsons, Pakistan 1997
- (Ed.) Francis Robinson, *The Cambridge Illustrated History of The Islamic World,* Cambridge University Press, 1996
- Edward S. Said, *Orientalism*, 1977, USA
- Ziauddin Sardar and Zafar Abbas Malik*, Muhammad (pbuh) for Beginners*, Icon, Cambridge 1994
- Ghulam Sarwar, *Islam - Beliefs and Teachings*, The Muslim Educational Trust, London 1994
- Jawed ul Haq Siddiqui, *21st Century & the Birth of United States of Islam*, USI Publications, Karachi 1997
- Idries Shah*, Reflections*, The Octagon Press, London MCMLXVIII
- The Sirdar Iqbal Ali Shah, *Muhammad: The Prophet*, Tracton UK 1996 (orig. 1932)
- (Ed.) Tahir Shah, *The Middle East Beside Book*, Octagon Press, 1991
- Desmond Stewart*, The Alhambra*, Reader's Digest Association, London & NEWSWEEK, New York, 1974
- Desmond Stewart, *Mecca*, NEWSWEEK, New York 1980
- William Montgomery Watt, *A Short History of Islam*, Oneworld, Oxford 1996

Published on Internet

- Abdul Hakim Murad, *Islam and the New Millennium*, Belfast, 1997
- Abu Iman 'Abd ar-Rahman Robert Squires, *Orientalism, Misinformation and Islam*, Florida 1998

Leaflet, Brochures and Magazines from

- Islamic Propagation Centre International, Durban, South Africa
- UKIM Da'wah Centre, Birmingham 1999
- The London Central Mosque, UK
- *Impact International,* London 1999
- *Common Sense*, Milton Keynes 1996
- *Khilafah*, London, 1998
- *Al-Furqan*, London 1998
- *Forum - Bulletin Forum for Social Studies*, London 1998
- *The Fountain*, London 1998
- *Al-Istiqaamah*, London 1998
- *Trends*, London 1998
- *Q-News International*, London 1998
- *TIME*, London 1999
- New Millennium Experience Company, *Millennium*, NMEC, London 1999
- The Sunday Times, *The Chronicle of the Future*, 1999

'May the peace and blessings be upon the Prophet (pbuh), upon his Family and his Companions. We pray that Allah, the Lord of Majesty and Beauty, blesses all those whose tireless efforts have tried to establish Allah's Kingdom upon the Earth. May Allah, Praise and Glory to Him, make them nearest to Him when the Appointed Hour comes.' Amin.

THE SPHERE OF STRANGE BUT TRUE

The most often used name in the world is Muhammad, which means 'The Praised One'.

The only wild camels in the world are in Australia. They were originally taken there by Muslims from Afghanistan, and provided early transport.

In the Middle Ages, the Latin Christians used to study the works of a sage whom they called Doctor Maximus. Many of them did not know that this was a translation of the Sufi teacher Ibn al-Arabi's title; 'Al-Sheikh al-Akbar'.

Alcohol was first distilled by the tenth-century alchemist Jabir ibn Hayyah, el-Sufi. The first translation of his work was by an Englishman, Robert of Chester, in 1144.

Chinese Muslims developed the art of combat and self-defense called Wushu. Muslims who excelled in Wushu such as Chang Yushun, Hu Dabai, Mu Ying, Lan Yu, Feng Shu and Ding Dexing helped Zhu Yuanzhang to establish the Qing Dynasty (1644-1911) during which the Muslims established various schools of Wushu.

The first historical study was made by Ibn Khaldun, born in Tunis in the fourteenth century. His Muqaddimah is still a classic.

Paper was brought to Europe by Arab Muslims from China.

Printing apparatus used in Afghanistan 1,000 years ago still exists.

Shakespeare uses stories found in Arabic; and Chaucer's 'Pear Tree' tale is found in the Persian of the Muslim Rumi.

Tabby (cat) is an Arabic word. So are filly, algebra, troubadour, admiral, traffic, cheque, tariff and magazine.

Frederick II of Sicily was so Arabised that he was called 'The Baptised Sultan.'

The British King Offa of Mercia (757-96) struck a dinar in gold with his name on it and 'There is no God but Allah' as a part of the inscription. One of these coins is in the British Museum.

The first book translated in England (The Dictes and Sayings of the Philosophers) is a translation from an Arabic work.

Arabic figures are the figures used in arithmetic (1,2, 3 etc.,) and transmitted to the West by Muslim Arab mathematicians, to replace the clumsy Roman Numerals, I, II, III, etc. Scholars have argued whether the Arabic name for the figures is Hindi (from India) or Hindasdi (engineering figures). The former explanation is the most favoured.

King John of England offered to become a Muslim and to hand over fealty of his kingdom to the Muslim Moors, if they would help him. The Muslim Moorish King refused the offer.

The first history of religions was written by Ibn Hazm of Cordoba (died 1064). He is honoured in the West as the founder of the discipline of comparative religion.

Freudian analysis theories of dreams were advanced by the Muslim Hakim Sanai of Ghazna (Afghanistan) . . . years before Sigmund Freud was born.

The claim that man is evolved and will continue to evolve is found in the works of Rumi, of Konia (Turkey) who died in 1273, year before Darwin.

The claim that immense power resides in the atom was made by the Muslim Shabistari, a Persian sage, who died in the 13th century, in his Secret Garden.

The 'Moors' of Andalusia were overwhelmingly Spanish in blood, having been converted to Islam by the Muslim Arabs.

The oldest university in the world is Al-Azhar, in Cairo, dating to 970 of the Christian Era. European universities like Oxford, mostly under Arabian influence, started to come into being in the twelfth century.

The great Franciscan teacher, Roger Bacon, lecturing at the then new University of Oxford in the thirteenth century, wore an Arabian robe and taught from Arab textbooks, on illuministic philosophy - mysticism - as well as Ptolemy and Euclid.

The star-and-crescent emblem is not an Islamic one: it was adopted by the Turks, when they conquered Byzantium, from the Christians. They, in turn, took it from Near-Eastern pagans.

THE MESSAGE OF JUSTICE TO ALL MANKIND

The Kingdom of Allah is coming. Peace to all these nations, with an Invitation to join as Muslims or as another Community.

'May the Peace, Blessing and Mercy of Allah be upon you'

Afghanistan
Albania
Algeria
Andorra
Angola
Anguilla
Antigua
Argentina
Armenia
Aruba
Australia
Austria
Azerbaijan
Bahamas
Bangladesh
Barbados
Belarus
Belgium
Belize
Benin
Bermuda
Bhutan
Bolivia
Bosnia-Herzgovina
Botswana
Brazil
Brunei
Bulgaria
Burkina Faso
Burma/ Myanmar
Burundi
Cambodia
Cameroon
Canada
Cape Verde
Cayman Islands
Central African
Republic
Ceuta
Chad
Chechnya
Chile
China
Christmas Islands
Cocos Islands
Columbia
Comoros
Congo D.R.
Congo R.
Cook Islands
Coral Sea Islands
Costa Rica
Cute d'Ivoire
Croatia
Cuba
Cyprus (Greek
Cyprus (Turkish)
Czech Republic
Dagestan
Denmark
Diego Garccia
Dijibouti
Dominica
Dominican
Republic
East Timor
Ecuador
Egypt
El Salvador
Equatorial Guinea
Eritrea
Estonia
Ethiopia
Faeroe Islands
Fiji
Finland
France
French Guinea
French Polynesia
Gabon
Gambia
Georgia
Germany
Ghana
Gibraltar
Greece
Greenland
Grenada
Guadeloupe
Guam
Guatemala
Guinea
Guinea-Bissau
Guyana
Haiti
Honduras
Hong Kong
Hungary
Iceland
India
Indonesia
Iran
Iraq
Israel
Italy
Jamaica
Jammu & Kashmir
Japan
Jordan
Kanaky/New
Caledonia
Kazakhstan
Kenya
Kiribtat
Korea
Korea, North
Korea, South
Kosovo
Kuwait
Kyrgyzstan
Laos
Latvia
Lebanon
Lesotho
Liberia
Libya
Liechtenstein
Lithuania
Luxembourg
Macau
Macedonia
Madagascar
Malawi
Malaysia
Maldives
Mali
Malta
Malvbinas/
Falkland Islands
Marshall Islands
Martinique
Mauritania
Mauritius
Mayotte
Melilla
Mexico
Micronesia
Moldova
Monaco
Mongolia
Montserrat
Morocco
Mozambique
Myanmar/ Burma
Namibia
Nauru
Nepal
Netherlands
Netherlands Antilles
New Zealand/
Aoteroa
Nicaragua
Niger
Nigeria
Niue
Norfolk Islands
Northern Marianas
Norway
Oman
Pakistan
Palau
Palestine
Panama
Papua Guinea
Paraguay
Peru
Phillipines
Pitcairn
Poland
Portugal
Puerto Rico
Qatar
Reunion
Romania
Russia
Rwanda
Sahara (Western)
St. Helena
St. Kitts-Nevis
St. Lucia
St. Pierre and
Miquelon
St. Vincent
Samoa
Samoa (America)
San Marino
Sao Tome and
Principe
Saudi Arabia
Senegal
Seychelles
Sierra Leone
Singapore
Slovakia
Slovenia
Solomon Is.
Somalia
Spain
Sri Lanka
Sudan
Suriname
Swaziland
Sweden
Switzerland
Syria
Tajikistan
Taiwan
Tanzania
Thailand
Tibet
Togo
Tokelau Is.
Tonga
Tunisia
Turkey
Turkmenistan
Turks & Caicos
Tuvalu
Uganda
Ukraine
United Arab
Emirates
United Kingdom of
Great Britain
United States of
America
Uruguay
Uzbekistan
Vanuatu
Vatican City
Venezuela
Vietnam
Virgin Is. (Am)
Virgin Is. (Br)
Wallis and Futuna
Yemen, Rep.
Yugoslavia Fed Rep
Zambia
Zimbabwe